School Leader Internship:

Developing, Monitoring, and Evaluating Your Leadership Experience

Gary E. Martin,
William F. Wright,
and Arnold B. Danzig

EYE ON EDUCATION
6 DEPOT WAY WEST, SUITE 106
LARCHMONT, NY 10538
(914) 833–0551
(914) 833–0761 fax
www.eyeoneducation.com

Library of Congress Cataloging-in-Publication Data

Martin, Gary E., 1949 July 16-
    School leader internship ; developing, monitoring, and evaluating your leadership experience / Gary E. Martin, William F. Wirght & Arnold B. Danzig.
       p. cm.
    Inclludes bibliographical references and index.
       ISBN 1-930556-65-9
       1. School administrators--Training of--United States. 2. School management and organization--Study and teaching (Internship)--United States. 1.Wright, William f., 1940-II. Danzig, Arnold Bob, 1948- III. Title.

    LB1738.5.M385 2004
    371.2'0071'5--dc21

    10 9 8 7 6 5 4 3 2 1

Editorial and production services provided by
Richard H. Adin Freelance Editorial Services
52 Oakwood Blvd., Poughkeepsie, NY 12603-4112
(914-471-3566)

Also Available from EYE ON EDUCATION

Internship Plan and Final Approval Page

The plan outlined in this text and other documentation is approved for meeting the requirements for the internship.

_____

Intern (Printed Name)

_____   _____

Intern Signature   Date

_____

Site Supervisor (Printed Name)

_____   _____

Site Supervisor Signature   Date

_____

University Supervisor (Printed Name)

_____   _____

University Supervisor Signature   Date

The internship is approved and meets all requirements of the University

_____   _____

University Supervisor Signature   Date

Foreword

School leaders have long identified the internship as the most important component of their training. University professors, district administrators, and graduate students all recognize how crucial the internship is. They all agree that prospective administrators can learn just so much in a classroom.

A truly meaningful internship would require an aspiring administrator to spend quality time with a mentoring administrator in a school or district setting. The more time, the better. The more involvement, the better. The more practical, hands-on learning experience, the better. Patient but steady monitoring and mentoring by a site-based administrator would be a plus. The ongoing involvement of a mentoring professor from the intern's department of educational administration would also strengthen the experience. And the only really effective way for graduate students in educational administration, their professors, and their potential employers to truly assess the aspiring administrators' knowledge and skills is to intern them in a realistic administrative setting. But is a meaningful internship possible, given all the obstacles?

Gary Martin, William Wright, and Arnold Danzig believe so, and they have written the handbook, *School Leadership Internship*, to demonstrate how to do it. The book is timely, now that the "Standards for School Leaders" developed by the Interstate School Leaders Licensure Consortium (ISLLC) are gradually becoming adopted by state licensure agencies and university preparation programs alike. The book also builds nicely on the recent release of new standards for departments of educational administration developed by the National Policy Board for Educational Administration (NPBEA) and implemented by the Educational Leaders Constituent Council (ELCC) in collaboration with the National Council on Accreditation of Teacher Education (NCATE). *School Leadership Internship* not only provides a roadmap for developing, monitoring, and evaluating the internship, it nicely dovetails these recommendations with the ISLLC and NCATE/ELCC standards.

The authors boldly begin with the general assumption that a quality internship is only possible if the student really, really wants to make it happen. In other words, the authors take the university and the school district off the hook for ensuring the student's successful internship. Instead, they place the onus on the aspiring administrators to develop and carry out meaningful on-the-job experiences pretty much on their own.

Preparing to be a school administrator was never intended to be simple or easy. Those students who never intend to become school leaders will probably dislike this book because what it recommends is a lot of practical and therefore, hard work. The authors clearly wrote this manual for the student who wants practical training to become a school leader. It provides such a student with a practical, step-by-step process to experience a quality internship. Future generations of school administrators will owe a debt of gratitude to Martin, Wright, and Danzig for having written this handbook.

E. Joseph Schneider, Deputy Executive Director
American Association of School Administrators

Note to the Instructor

This manual can be adapted to a variety of needs. It is written as a stand-alone text for a yearlong capstone internship. Depending on the nature of your institution's program, it may be used for a one-semester internship, field experiences used throughout a certification or masters program, or a combination of experiences in various required courses and the concluding internship. It can serve as a stand-alone internship text or as supplemental material. You may require students to complete all or part of the manual and/or provide the student with specific university requirements in a handout format to supplement and guide the use of the text.

A brief list of the unique aspects of the text is provided for your consideration:

Self, Peer, and Superior Assessments. Requires the student to plan according to individual needs, experiences, and goals. Allows the intern to focus on specific strengths or areas needing improvement.

School/District Assessments. Requires the student to plan according to school or district needs and goals. Allows the intern to serve the district as he/she works on individual professional development.

Internship Plan Report. Requires the student to analyze, prepare, and present a professional report. Allows the intern to take a leadership role in the development of the internship.

Project. Requires the intern to lead. Allows the intern to utilize all the leadership skill areas, as opposed to observation and/or carrying out assigned tasks.

38 Skill and Experience areas. Requires the student to learn and perform in a variety of essential school contexts. Allows the intern a breadth of experience.

Theory into Practice. Requires the student to apply learning from previous coursework. Allows the intern the opportunity to reflect and form effective habits and increase their learning from the field of educational research. This section is provided for review and focus, not to supplant previous instruction and study.

Interviews. Requires the student to gather additional information and an overall perspective from leaders in various positions in the school or district. Allows the intern to develop a network and gain insights and additional vital activities for various administrative/curricular areas. Interviews are recommended at the beginning of the internship.

Reflective Practice. Requires the student to learn the art of reflection and learning from practice. Allows the intern to develop a necessary skill and begin effective reflection in practice, as well as on practice.

Future Professional Development. Requires the student to analyze and evaluate his or her experience. Allows the intern to and plan for further development.

Vita and Letter of Application. Requires the student to develop a professional "accomplishment oriented" vita and relevant letter of application. Allows the intern to develop needed documentation for future leadership position.

Final Report. Requires the student to analyze, evaluate, develop, and present a concluding professional report. Allows the intern the opportunity to take a leadership role in the evaluation of the internship and demonstrate the knowledge and skill gained from the experience.

Use of Site Supervisors. The role of the site supervisor is crucial and at the discretion of the university instructor. We recommend supervisors take an active part in assisting the intern in planning, monitoring, implementing, and evaluating the internship. The role of the site supervisor should be developed and communicated to both the site supervisor and intern.

The authors hope the comprehensiveness and flexibility of the text will support and assist you in "raising the bar" for your internship and meeting/exceeding the ISLLC and ELCC standards.

TABLE OF CONTENTS

Introducing School Leader Internship

To the Intern

This text will serve as a guide for developing, monitoring, and evaluating your planned experience. It differs greatly from previous internships where the new leader waited for assigned tasks or was given a limited range of opportunity to grow and develop. Now, you will be challenged in each of the 10 essential skill areas and a wide variety of contexts. You will plan, perform, reflect, and form new and better leadership skill habits in:

- Creating and managing the vision

- Making good decisions

- Communicating effectively

- Using appropriate style and power

- Leading groups

- Motivating others

- Resolving conflicts and issues

- Creating a positive culture and climate

- Leading change

- Conducting meaningful evaluation

You will develop, refine, and improve these skills, along with gaining new knowledge in a vast spectrum of school contexts. Examples of the differing contexts are staff development, classroom instruction, budgeting, transportation, food service, technology, and others that will make up the 38 leadership and skill areas. You will meet and learn from a wide variety of individuals from the personnel director, athletic director, principal, superintendent, and board members to leaders in the community.

How challenging your experience will be is up to you. Like the old adage, "You get out of it what you put into it," you are urged to raise the bar and seek a true challenge for several very important reasons. First, you will be observed during your experience, and others will clearly see the rigor and expectations you set for yourself. Second, there may be no other time when so many other leaders will take the time to teach, counsel, and assist you in your learning. Most important, we are depending on your leadership to better educate the next generation of our society.

Overview of the Internship

Stage 1: Assessment

- Choose the school/district site and supervisor.
- Write the vita.
- Complete the ISLLC assessments.
- Gather other assessments and evaluations.
- Write statements of your position and leadership goals.
- Obtain and analyze school/district assessments, improvement plans, etc.
- Analyze the vita and assessments for strengths and weaknesses; summarize the main points; prioritize areas of focus.

Stage 2: Plan

- Choose one or more activities in each of the 38 skill and experience areas.
- Meet with site supervisor to reach consensus on the planned activities and plan local project(s) and various service activities.
- Decide which individuals to work with, observe and interview them, and then compile a networking list of these contacts.
- Organize the notebook used to document the internship.
- Make a professional presentation of the overall plan to the site-supervisor and university supervisor, if applicable.

Stage 3: Implementation

- Implement planned activities and keep documentation.

- Conduct interviews.
- Practice the 10 major skills.
- Reflect on practice.
- Keep a journal.
- Keep a log of activities.
- Monitor progress and adjust the activities throughout this stage.

Stage 4: Evaluation

- Write a brief summary/evaluation for each of the 38 skill and experience areas.
- Write a summary of reflection on practice and the 10 major skill areas.
- Compile a prioritized list of school/district improvements and recommendations.
- Develop a portfolio.
- Update the vita.
- Write a letter of application.
- Write a Future Professional Development Plan.
- Present the Final Internship Report to the site-supervisor and university supervisor, if applicable.

Background/Recommendations for Change

"Criticism of the ways in which men and women are prepared for school leadership positions enjoys a long history. Perhaps the only things more depressing than an honest appraisal of current educational administration programs is the knowledge that so little progress has been made in resolving the deeply ingrained weaknesses that have plagued training systems for so long" (Murphy, 1992, p.79). The literature is replete with calls for reform and improvement (AASA, 1960; Kaplan, 1989; Barth, 1990; Muse and Thomas, 1991; Milstein, Bobroff, & Restine, 1991; Jacobson, 1996; Forsyth, 1998).

Advocates for administrative training reform value field experience highly, particularly the internship experience (NAESP, 1990, p. 38). NAESP states:

> Over the years the academic tracks for the preparation of principals and superintendents have differed only slightly, if at all. In this sense, school administrator preparation programs might well be character-

ized as generic. Many of the administrative skills essential for success are, in fact, generic to preparation for the elementary principal, the secondary principal, and the superintendent. Such skills should be consistently taught and reinforced in administrator preparation programs. However, the day-to-day activities of each of these leaders vary significantly. It is therefore equally apparent that preparation programs for elementary and middle school principals should be redesigned so as to be much more position-specific (p. 22). The structure and contribution of clinical experiences should be studied further with the goal of providing richer practical components in programs for aspiring principals (p. 38).

Patrick Forsyth (1998) states "Commission reports, research, and other critiques and reform reports of the last decade have raised serious questions about conventional assumptions and practices, concurring that preparation programs for school administration must confront the issues that confront school administration." Recommendations from these sources commonly include:

1. Key stakeholders (schools, universities, and professional associations) to share responsibility for and collaborate in preparing school leaders

2. Preparation programs to balance professional knowledge with relevant administrator craft knowledge, especially in the area of curriculum, teaching, and learning

3. Restructuring the professional preparation process to take into account how adults learn

4. Changes based on the recognition that clinical experiences are a vital part of administrator preparation (p. 7)

Jacobson (1996) concluded, "Conventional wisdom suggests that if you continue to do what you have always done, you can expect to get what you always got" (p. 271). Addressing the criticisms and calls for reform, many of the leading educational organizations have responded with standards for programs and practice for school leaders. These include:

- American Association of Colleges for Teacher Education (1988)

- American Association of School Administrators (1960, 1983, 1993, and Hoyle, English, & Steffy 1998)

- National Association of Elementary School Principals (1990)

- National Association of Secondary School Principals (1985)

- National Commission on Excellence in Educational Administration (1987)

- National Council for Accreditation for Teacher Education (1982, 1994, 1995)

- National Council for Professors of Educational Administration (2000)

- National Policy Board for Educational Administration (1993)

- University Council for Educational Administration (1987).

The numerous standards recommended by these organizations can be distilled to the following nine characteristics of an effective internship experience:

1. Clear objectives

2. Adequate planning, supervision, and follow-up

3. Problem-centered and project-centered experiences

4. Experiences that meet individual needs and goals

5. Relevance to actual and specific job demands

6. Higher-level activities (leading, deciding, resolving, reflecting, etc.)

7. University and school district collaboration

8. Quality candidates, including more women and minorities

9. High standards that are supported nationally

Purpose of the Text

School Leader Internship: Developing, Monitoring, and Evaluating Your Leadership Experience was written to meet the general standards above and the specific ISLLC standards to assist aspiring educational leaders in the assessment, design, implementation, and evaluation of a university internship or district leadership development experience. The term *leadership experience* is appropriate and signifies a radical departure from the traditional internship and/or district training program. In using a leadership development approach, the intern assumes the leadership role. In effect, it becomes a self-strategic plan requiring assessments, timelines, allocation of resources, benchmarks, ongoing monitoring and adjusting, evaluation, and reporting.

The internship is both a capstone of educational endeavor and a beginning experience in meeting the demands of a new position in educational leadership. It is assumed that prerequisite knowledge and skill are at an adequate level for entry into the new leadership experience. The internship requires a high level of knowledge, skill, and effort. The experience of leadership is the goal. The administrator must assume responsibility to be effective in the internship.

Warren Bennis (1989) echoed this sentiment as "What is true for leaders is, for better or for worse, true for each of us: we are our own raw material. Only when we know what we're made of and what we want to make of it can we begin our lives—and we must do it despite an unwitting conspiracy of people and events against us." The intern becomes accountable for the breadth, depth, and rigor of the experience. True leaders welcome this responsibility and the resulting balance of authority that allow them to accomplish great things.

The intern is responsible for assessing, designing, implementing, and evaluating an experience that:

- Meets the intern's individual needs
- Provides an adequate breadth of experience
- Sets high standards/expectations
- Connects research/theory and practice
- Provides a service to the district/school
- Develops a global perspective
- Incorporates assessment and reflection
- Provides experience and evidence to gain the desired administrative position
- Is a quality experience

In a four-year study (Martin, Wright, Perry, & Amick 2000) of the use of the first published *Intern Manual* (Martin & Wright 1995), both supervising administrators and interns rated the *Manual* highly for its usefulness in the nine aspects listed above.

This text, however, is only a guide, and the final project outcome will remain the challenge and responsibility of the intern. University and/or district supervisors work collaboratively with the intern on the design, final assessment, and evaluation of the internship development experience.

Standards

The text is designed to meet the standards set by the Interstate School Leaders Licensure Consortium (ISLLC). The ISLLC was organized under the Council of Chief State School Officers and the National Policy Board of Educational Administration in part to identify and establish a set of common professional standards for school leaders. It was felt that a set of common standards would provide an avenue for improvement efforts in a variety of areas of administrative leadership. "The standards set out to improve school leadership by improving the quality of programs that prepare school leaders while establishing a level of accountability of the efforts of these programs" (Murphy, Shipman, & Pearlman, 1997).

The ISLLC Standards for School Leaders (CCSSO, 1996) has become the national standard and was adopted in most states. This is because of its quality, comprehensiveness, and acceptance by many of our nation's leading school administrative organizations and accrediting agencies. The new millennium has ushered in a sense of working cooperatively to better prepare school leaders (NCPEA, 2000).

The intern must be knowledgeable of the professional associations that provide the guidance and resources for effective school leadership. Although supportive of the ISLLC standards, each association may offer additional standards, competencies, proficiencies, and other resources to assist school leaders in a particular field. It is strongly recommended that the intern become an active member in the professional associations of his/her choice for continued and further professional development. Appendices A.3-A.5 list the standards and proficiencies for these associations.

The ISLLC standards set high benchmarks for the intern to meet. Many are standards that can only be attained following full-time administrative positions. The internship, however, will be the beginning for meeting the standards. Generally, the six ISLLC standards expect the aspiring administrator to:

- ♦ Lead with vision

- ♦ Create a culture/climate for student and faculty growth

- ♦ Manage effectively

- ♦ Work collaboratively with the community

- ♦ Act with integrity and an ethical manner

- ♦ Take part in and respond to the larger political, economic, social, legal, and cultural community

ISLLC outlines the requisite knowledge, disposition, and performance to attain each of the six standards.

In addition, the intern must use effective habits in the planning and implementation of the internship project. Utilizing reflective practice in the monitoring and evaluation phases is also required. The intern should be cognizant of the intent to begin to master these goals and begin gathering evidence of accomplishment.

Meeting the 7th Standard

The National Council for the Accreditation of Teacher Education (NCATE) is used by many universities for accreditation and serves as the premier organization for setting standards for university leadership development programs. At the direction of NCATE, which was updating its entire review process, the National Policy Board for Educational Administration began the task of rewriting its original standards for the review of departments of educational administration. Each of the 11-member associations that make up the Policy Board were invited to nominate one person to serve on a "working group" to develop the revised NCATE standards. The resulting group consisted of two association representatives (from the Association for Supervision and Curriculum Development and the National Association for Elementary School Principals) and six professors of educational administration selected by the American Association of Colleges of Teacher Education, American Association of School Administrators, Council of Chief State School Officers, National Association of Secondary School Principals, the National Council of Professors of Educational Administration, and the University Council of Educational Administration.

Neither NCATE nor the National School Boards Association selected representatives to the working group. Joe Schneider, executive secretary of the NPBEA, was the staff director for the working group. When it finished its assignment, both the NPBEA and eventually NCATE adopted the new standards for the review of departments of educational administration. At that point, they were turned over to the Educational Leaders Constituent Council (ELCC), which actually conducts the review and recommends "national recognition" to those departments that satisfactorily meet the standards. The ELCC, an ongoing project of the NPBEA and is funded and managed by a consortium of NPBEA members: ASCD, AASA, NAESP, and NASSP.

The National Policy Board and NCATE approved the ELCC standards. The standards include the six ISLLC standards and a new seventh standard: "A school administrator is an educational leader who promotes the success of all students by substantial, sustained, standards-based experiences in real settings that are planned and guided cooperatively by university and school district personnel for graduate credit." The text meets this standard for universities as well as high standards for district administrative development programs.

Outline of the Text

Stage One covers the necessary personal and district/school assessments. These include:

♦ Vita development and assessment

♦ ISLLC knowledge and performance assessment

♦ ISLLC dispositions assessment

♦ District/school assessment and/or improvement plans

- ◆ Any additional personal assessments
- ◆ Leadership and Position Goals

Stage Two covers the development of the plan. A variety of experience and skill areas are listed under each of the ISLLC standards. Suggested activities are listed for each experience and skill area. The intern may choose from these activities or may design other activities related to the area. The intern will be required to work in every experience and skill area. He/she is NOT required to undertake all of the suggested activities listed. In this fashion, the internship plan can be individualized while ensuring a sufficient broad base of experience and high level of expectation. The final part of this section is the design of a local district/school project.

Stage Three covers the implementation of the plan. This section addresses interviewing, putting theory into practice, reflection in and on practice, keeping a log or a journal, and monitoring and formative evaluation.

Stage Four covers the evaluation and the final internship report. This includes the summative evaluation, reflection, and recommendations for the district/school and individual further professional development.

Outcomes

The intern will have accomplish the following by the end of the internship:

- ◆ Conducted a self- and district/school assessment
- ◆ Developed a Vita or professional resume
- ◆ Begun the development of a professional portfolio
- ◆ Composed a letter of application
- ◆ Designed a three-year professional development plan
- ◆ Compiled a network of resources
- ◆ Experienced the art of reflective practice and effective habits
- ◆ Progressed in his/her current knowledge, disposition, and skill performance
- ◆ Gained a leadership experience covering a wide variety of areas

Acknowledgements

Thanks to all the interns, supervisors, and faculty that assisted with recommendations for this text. A very special thanks to Vanessa Naylon for editing, indexing, typing, and keeping us moving on this project. All your efforts are greatly appreciated.

Stage One

Internship Assessment

The first step in developing a plan for individual and school improvement is to assess the need for improvement or change. In this part, the intern must gather and analyze various personal and district/school documents. These include a current vita, ISLLC self-assessments, other self-assessments and evaluations, and district/school improvement and/or strategic plans. The intern will also compile a list of available resources.

The following sections further explain the needed documentation. The final section provides guidelines for analysis and reporting.

1.1 Development and Assessment of the Vita

The intern must complete a draft of his/her vita during the assessment phase of the internship. A vita lists the facts of past education, experience, and accomplishments. It will be used for learning and planning for the internship and future professional development. The vita can then be reviewed to note knowledge, experience, and accomplishments in specific leadership areas as well as inexperience in other vital leadership areas. The internship will be cited and added to the vita at the end of the internship.

The following recommendations and format will guide the intern through the development of an appropriate and powerful accomplishment-oriented vita. The guidelines for the vita are as follows:

- Well-defined categories/sections in appropriate order
- Qualifications and preferences match the position desired
- Neat and conservative (on white or beige paper, more space than type)
- Accurate and ethical
- Accomplishment oriented
- Results of accomplishments shown, if any (supportive evidence in portfolio)

1

- Information outside of professional life omitted
- Clear, readable font (12-point for most fonts)
- Grammatically correct (consistent use of past-tense verbs)
- Several pages in length (not a one-page business resume)

Preferred Order of Categories

Choose the categories that are most accurate, ethical and appropriate. Other categories or combinations of these and others for unique individuals and/or experiences may be used.

Heading

Education/certification

Administrative, supervisory, and/or leadership experience

Teaching experience

Coaching experience (if applicable)

Related experience (if applicable)

Other experience (if applicable)

Professional development

Publications and/or presentations and/or grants (if applicable)

Curriculum experience (if applicable)

Professional affiliations

Honors and/or awards (if applicable)

Community involvement/service

Professional references

Reference page

Sample Heading

Ian Tern
123 4th Street, Phoenix, AZ 85352
(W) (602) 555–6711, (H) (602) 555–6712, Intern@isp.com

Heading Guidelines

a. Heading should be three lines in length.

b. Name should **stand out** and be legal name.

c. Provide complete address, phone number(s) with area codes, and e-mail.

Sample Education/Certification Category

Education/Certification

M.Ed. Northern Arizona University, Flagstaff, AZ., 2000, Educational Leadership

Texas A&M University, College Station, TX, 1996–98 (30 hours), Business Administration

BA Northern Arizona University, Flagstaff, AZ., 1995, Elementary Education,

Superintendent Certificate—Arizona (in progress)

Principal Certificate—Arizona

Teacher Certificate—K–8 Physical Education, Arizona

Special Education—K–12 Endorsement, Arizona

Category Guidelines

a. Degree should be highlighted (placed in margin as above).

b. Following degree is area of degree, institution, city, state, and year awarded.

c. Major and/or minor may be listed, if appropriate and useful.

d. Address of institution is not needed.

e. Note any significant amount of hours taken not leading to degree (as shown above).

f. Skip one line to separate certificates from degrees.

g. Certificates are cited exactly as written on certificate and include name of state.

h. List administrative certificate(s) first.

i. Place any endorsements after teaching certificates.

j. Include current certification sought—use (in progress) or (expected completion date, that is, month and year).

Sample Administrative Experience Category

Administrative Experience

♦ Principal, Kennedy High School, Northside ISD, Tampa, FL, 1983–89

♦ Administered the overall alternative school program for ED and LD special education students, grades 6–12

♦ Designed and implemented new rigorous academic program, which resulted in increased attendance from 68% to 85%, increased passing rate from under 50% to over 85%, and decreased serious behavior violations from 75 per year to less than 10 per year

♦ Expanded academic offerings to include gifted classes, drug education, advisory and cooperative work, and learning programs

♦ Trained staff in learning theory, behavior and crisis management, effective instructional strategies, and collaborative planning

♦ Wrote, implemented, and evaluated the Social Skills Curriculum in two-year doctoral study

---

Sample Leadership Category

Leadership Experience

♦ Mathematics Department Chair, Parker High School, Waco, TX, 1997–present

♦ Chaired all department meetings

♦ Served on district math curriculum committee

♦ Supervised the textbook adoption committee

♦ Assisted principal in math department budget development and evaluation

---

Category Guidelines

a. Use Administrative Experience category only if you were certified and served in an administrative position. It is unethical to invent a title, for example, assistant principal, if you only assisted the principal.

b. Use Supervisory Experience category only if you were certified and served in a supervisory position (supervising adults).

c. Use Leadership Experience category for all other leadership roles, for example, department or grade level chair, committee chair, site council member, etc.

d. Categories are combinable, for example, supervisory/leadership experience, if experienced in both.

e. List title first, then school, city, state, and date(s).

f. Use bullets and relevant past-tense verbs for all accomplishments, for example, wrote, implemented, supervised, etc.

g. List any results of accomplishment, if known and appropriate.

h. Use two to six bullets under each title.

Sample Teaching Experience Category

Teaching Experience

♦ Third Grade Teacher—Otondo Elementary, Yuma Elementary District #1, Yuma, AZ, 1998

♦ Planned and taught lessons in math, language arts, and science

♦ Implemented Cooperative Discipline system and observed positive growth in social behavior in most students

♦ Served on reading curriculum evaluation team and assisted in the development of the revised curriculum

♦ Sponsored and tutored academic decathlon team that placed second in district competition

♦ Attended district classroom computer training

Coaching Experience
Related Experience
Other Experience

(Same format as in "Teaching Experience" above)

Category Guidelines

a. Use Coaching Experience category if duty was contracted and experience was significant. List minor coaching duties as bullet(s) under Teaching Experience category

b. Use Related Experience category if duties are related to teaching/administrative duties

c. Use Other Experience category if significant experience, for example, former career, etc.

d. Capitalize and list title first, then organization or school, city, state, and date(s)

e. Use bullets and relevant past-tense verbs, for example, wrote, implemented, supervised, etc.

f. List any results of accomplishments, if known

g. Use two to six bullets, typically more if very recent or significant number of years in the following format:

Title, organization or school, city, state, date(s)

- Past-tense verb + accomplishment

- Past tense verb + accomplishment

- Past-tense verb + accomplishment

- Past-tense verb + accomplishment

Sample Professional Development Category

Professional Development

Aspiring Principals Workshop, Arizona School Administrators, Phoenix, AZ, June, 1999 Using Computers for Learning, Emily Drake, Inc., Mesa, AZ, 1998 (30 hours)

Category Guidelines

a. For fewer than two citations, indent with bullet under title.

b. There is no limit to the number of citations in this category.

c. All training cited should be relevant to education/leadership.

d. Note number of hours (if a significant amount).

e. Cite the title first, then organization, city, state, and date(s).

Sample Presentations and/or Publications Category (if applicable)

Presentations

Tern, I. N. (1995, November). *Using manipulatives in the classroom.* Presentation for the Kyle District Inservice, Phoenix, AZ.

Publications

Tern, I. N. (1999, September 15). Parents helping in schools. *The Arizona Republic.* p. A12.

Category Guidelines

a. Cite all presentations and/or publications in APA or other appropriate format.

b. For five or fewer citations, use combination of categories; if more than five and at least two in each, use separate presentation and publication categories.

c. Be sure to include all coauthors or copresenters.

d. Consider citing dissertations, theses, and locally published curricular materials.

Sample Professional Affiliations Category

Professional Affiliations

Association for Supervision and Curriculum Development, 1988–present
Phi Delta Kappa, 1990–present, vice president, 1997
Arizona Educators Association, 1984–1995
Greater Miami Educational Foundation, 1998–present

Category Guidelines

a. Cite all current memberships in professional organizations.

b. Note any offices held.

c. Cite membership in any professional organizations of significant duration.

d. Spell out complete names of organizations—do not use acronyms.

Sample Honors/Awards/Scholarship Category

Awards/Scholarships

Teacher of the Year, Odessa Rotary, Odessa, TX, 1998
Phi Beta Gamma Outstanding Student Award, Northern Arizona University Chapter, Flagstaff, AZ, 1996

Category Guidelines

a. Use relevant category if you have two or more citations—otherwise, list under teaching or administrative category.

b. Use combination of categories, if appropriate (as in sample above).

c. Cite honor, award, or scholarship, then organization, city, state, and
    date.

Sample Civic/Community Service Category (optional)

Civic/Community Service
Scout Troop Leader, Troop 38, Mesa, AZ, 1991–1998
Everyone Reads Volunteer, Mesa Public Library, Mesa, AZ, 1998

Category Guidelines

a. List title, organization, city, state, and date(s).

b. Service should be related to goals or duties of the education profession instead of purely personal.

c. Service to a particular church or religion may be used or viewed as personal information and should not be cited.

Sample References Category

References
References will be included on the following page, if requested

Category Guidelines

a. Use as last category on vita.

b. It is unethical to include references with vita, unless references requested.

c. Be sure references have given permission to use their names.

Sample References Page

References
Dr. Bill Hickok, Principal
Page Elementary
184 Avenue C
Tombstone, AZ 85365
(520) 783–9999 / bh@isp.edu

Reference Page Guidelines

a. List name and title first.

b. List name of school or organization next.

c. List complete address, city, state, and zip code.

d. List phone number with area code and e-mail address.

e. This MUST be a separate page.

f. Cite no more than six references.

g. Must have reference for each place worked—if more than six, stay within last 10 years.

h. Try to use administrator references–personal references are not appropriate

i. Cite references in order of priority—often only the first three are contacted.

Frequently Asked Questions

1. Shouldn't the vita be organized by years, with the years in the left margin?

   No. That is a style used for a business resume, not an educational vita.

2. Should I use expensive paper with bright colors to make it stand out?

   Neither expensive nor inexpensive paper is necessary, but you should use a good-quality paper. Brightly colored paper is a tactic used in the world of business. Your experience and accomplishments should stand out, not the color of the paper.

3. What if I have gaps of time in my vita?

   You should exercise good judgment in this case. Often those with gaps in their career are raising children or tending to a sick family member or some other reasonable use of their time. There are others, however, who were fired and could not get another job, were in drug rehabilitation, or some other very personal reason. The point is that the reviewer of your resume may have doubts about which group you are in. Thus, unless your reasons are extremely personal, it is recommended that you provide some explanation for gaps in time to prevent the doubts of prospective employers.

4. I do not have much in the Leadership category. Should I list "leading students" in various activities or groups?

Your inexperience with leadership should motivate you to volunteer or apply for positions that will give you the necessary experience. Do not wait for an administrative position to gain leadership experience. There are many committees to chair, councils to serve on, and programs to lead while still teaching. Use your vita as a learning experience and start filling in the gaps.

5. What if my coaching experience is quite extensive?

This is another judgment call. Much will depend on the position you are applying for. If, for example, you are applying for an assistant principal/athletic director position, then a complete listing of your coaching experience would be appropriate. If you were applying for solely an assistant principal position, then you would limit your Coaching Experience category and use as much as appropriate in the Leadership Experience category. Many duties and responsibilities in athletics leadership are the same as in school administration.

6. What if I do not belong to any professional organizations?

It's time to join! Choose what is appropriate to your career goals. Superintendents may join the American Association of School Administrators (AASA), secondary principals may join the National Association of Secondary School Administrators (NASSP), elementary principals may join the National Association of Elementary Principals (NAESP), and those interested in curriculum development may join the Association for Supervision and Curriculum Development (ASCD). It is recommended that you also become active in the state affiliations for these professional organizations and read their journals regularly. Again, you do not have to wait to get the position to learn more about the position.

7. What if I do not have any awards or honors?

Many great educators never received any honors or awards. Others were honored or recognized after their career ended. Honors and awards are bestowed on you by others—do not seek awards or honors, but graciously accept them.

8. Should I or shouldn't I list church activities?

In public education, we are bound by separation of church and state. Although active involvement with a particular church may denote many positive aspects of your service and character, it may also be viewed by some as interfering with the goals of public education. This is another judgment you must make.

With your vita, letter of application, and interview, your responsibility is to clearly show the prospective school district who you are.

This is your half of the work leading up to the contract. If your religious affiliation is such a big part of you that it goes with you into school, then it would be appropriate to cite your church work. If your religious affiliation is more personal in nature and is not brought into the school, then omitting it from your professional vita would be appropriate.

9. Why must the reference page be separate?

    Persons willing to provide reference information for you are assuming that only districts very interested in hiring you will contact them. They should not have to provide information to every district where you applied. Therefore, it is considered unethical to provide references unless requested in the job announcement or by the employer.

10. Why list accomplishments?

    Leaders accomplish things! This includes all educational leaders, especially teachers. A vita that shows only where and when you worked does not give any indication of accomplishment. Did you simply show up every day, or did you set goals and accomplish them? Accomplishment-oriented vitas do a much better job of showing who the leaders are. You should spend time analyzing your accomplishments (often forgotten or taken for granted) and use them for learning and setting future goals.

11. Is the vita changeable?

    Although one cannot change the facts, one can add facts and/or present them differently. One designs the resume according to the position sought. For example, the district may desire curricular experience for the position. In this case, an applicant could include a Curriculum Experience category and place it higher up in the list of categories used. Another example is a district that wants primary experience. In this case, the intern adds student teaching to the vita (normally not included) because that was the intern's only primary experience. In short, you should try to match your vita with the position.

1.2 Self-Assessment of ISLLC Knowledge and Performance Skills

The following section is a self-assessment instrument for measuring your knowledge and experience in each of the ISLLC standards. The intern should complete it as accurately and honestly as possible. Your choices are:

HD (high degree); SD (some degree); LD (low degree); or None

ISLLC Standard 1

A school administrator is an educational leader who promotes the success of all students by facilitating the *development, articulation, implementation,* and *stewardship* of a *vision of learning* that is *shared* and *supported* by the school community.

Your degree of knowledge and understanding of:

Learning goals in a pluralistic society	HD	SD	LD	None
Principles of developing and implementing strategic plans	HD	SD	LD	None
Systems theory	HD	SD	LD	None
Information sources, data collection, and analysis strategies	HD	SD	LD	None
Effective communication	HD	SD	LD	None
Effective consensus-building and negotiation skills	HD	SD	LD	None

Your skill/experience with processes and activities ensuring that:

Vision and mission of the school are effectively communicated to staff, parents, students, and community	HD	SD	LD	None
Vision and mission are communicated through use of symbols, ceremonies, stories, and similar activities	HD	SD	LD	None
Core beliefs of the school vision are modeled for all stakeholders	HD	SD	LD	None

Vision is developed with and among stakeholders	HD	SD	LD	None
Contributions of school community members to the realization of the vision are recognized and celebrated	HD	SD	LD	None
Progress toward the vision and mission is communicated to all stakeholders	HD	SD	LD	None
School community is involved in school improvement efforts	HD	SD	LD	None
The vision shapes the educational programs, plans, actions	HD	SD	LD	None
An implementation plan is developed in which objectives and strategies to achieve the vision/goals are clearly articulated	HD	SD	LD	None
Assessment data related to student learning are used to develop the school vision and goals	HD	SD	LD	None
Relevant demographic data pertaining to students and their families are used in developing the school mission and goals	HD	SD	LD	None
Barriers to achieving the vision are identified, clarified, and addressed	HD	SD	LD	None
Needed resources are sought and obtained to support the implementation of the school mission and goals	HD	SD	LD	None
Existing resources are used in support of the school vision and goals	HD	SD	LD	None
Vision, mission, and implementation plans are regularly monitored, evaluated, and revised	HD	SD	LD	None

ISLLC Standard 2

A school administrator is an educational leader who promotes the success of all students by *advocating, nurturing,* and *sustaining* a *school culture* and *instructional program* conducive to *student learning* and *staff professional growth.*

Your degree of knowledge and understanding of:

Student growth and development	HD	SD	LD	None
Applied learning theories	HD	SD	LD	None
Curriculum design, implementation, evaluation, refinement	HD	SD	LD	None
Principles of effective instruction	HD	SD	LD	None
Measurement, evaluation, and assessment strategies	HD	SD	LD	None
Diversity and its meaning for educational programs	HD	SD	LD	None
Adult learning and professional development models	HD	SD	LD	None
Change process for systems, organizations, and individuals	HD	SD	LD	None
Role of technology in promoting student learning and professional growth	HD	SD	LD	None
School cultures	HD	SD	LD	None

Your skill/experience with processes and activities ensuring that:

All individuals are treated with fairness, dignity, and respect	HD	SD	LD	None
Professional development promotes a focus on student learning consistent with the school vision and goals	HD	SD	LD	None
Students and staff feel valued and important	HD	SD	LD	None
Responsibilities and contributions of each individual are acknowledged	HD	SD	LD	None
Barriers to student learning are identified, clarified, and addressed	HD	SD	LD	None
Diversity is considered in developing learning experiences	HD	SD	LD	None

Lifelong learning is encouraged and modeled	HD	SD	LD	None
Culture of high expectations exists for self, student, and staff performance	HD	SD	LD	None
Technologies are used in teaching and learning	HD	SD	LD	None
Student and staff accomplishments are recognized and celebrated	HD	SD	LD	None
Multiple opportunities to learn are available to all students	HD	SD	LD	None
School is organized and aligned for success	HD	SD	LD	None
Curricular, cocurricular, and extracurricular programs are designed, implemented, evaluated, and refined	HD	SD	LD	None
Curriculum decisions are based on research, expertise of teachers, and the recommendations of learned societies	HD	SD	LD	None
School culture and climate are assessed on a regular basis	HD	SD	LD	None
A variety of sources of information regarding performance is used by staff and students	HD	SD	LD	None
Pupil personnel programs are developed to meet the needs of students and their families	HD	SD	LD	None

ISLLC Standard 3

A school administrator is an educational leader who promotes the success of all students by ensuring *management* of the *organization, operations,* and *resources* for a safe, efficient, and effective *learning environment.*
Your degree of knowledge and understanding of:

Theories and models of organizations and the principles of organizational development	HD	SD	LD	None
Operational procedures at the school and district level	HD	SD	LD	None
Principles and issues relating to school safety and security	HD	SD	LD	None

Human resources management and development	HD	SD	LD	None
Principles and issues relating to fiscal operations of school management	HD	SD	LD	None
Principles and issues relating to school facilities and use of space	HD	SD	LD	None
Legal issues impacting school operations	HD	SD	LD	None
Current technologies that support management functions	HD	SD	LD	None

Your skill/experience with processes and activities ensuring that:

Knowledge of learning, teaching, and student development is used to inform management decisions	HD	SD	LD	None
Operational procedures are designed and managed to maximize opportunities for successful learning	HD	SD	LD	None
Emerging trends are recognized, studied, and applied as appropriate	HD	SD	LD	None
Operational plans and procedures to achieve the vision and goals of the school are in place	HD	SD	LD	None
Collective bargaining and other contractual agreements related to the school are effectively managed	HD	SD	LD	None
School plant, equipment, and support systems operate safely, efficiently, and effectively	HD	SD	LD	None
Time is managed to maximize attainment of organizational goals	HD	SD	LD	None
Potential problems and opportunities are identified	HD	SD	LD	None
Problems are confronted and resolved in a timely manner	HD	SD	LD	None

Financial, human, and material resources are aligned to the goals of schools	HD	SD	LD	None
School acts in an enterprising way to support continuous improvement	HD	SD	LD	None
Organizational systems are regularly monitored and modified as needed	HD	SD	LD	None
Stakeholders are involved in decisions affecting schools	HD	SD	LD	None
Responsibility is shared to maximize ownership and accountability	HD	SD	LD	None
Effective problem-framing and problem-solving skills used	HD	SD	LD	None
Effective conflict resolution skills are used	HD	SD	LD	None
Effective group-process and consensus building skills are used	HD	SD	LD	None
Effective communication skills are used	HD	SD	LD	None
Technology is used effectively to manage school operations	HD	SD	LD	None
Fiscal resources of the school are managed responsibly, efficiently, and effectively	HD	SD	LD	None
A safe, clean, and aesthetically pleasing school environment is created and maintained	HD	SD	LD	None
Human resource functions support the attainment of school goals	HD	SD	LD	None
Confidentiality & privacy of school records are maintained	HD	SD	LD	None

ISLLC Standard 4

A school administrator is an educational leader who promotes the success of all students by *collaborating* with families and community members, *responding* to diverse community interests and needs, and *mobilizing community resources.*

Your degree of knowledge and understanding of:

Emerging issues and trends that potentially impact the school community	HD	SD	LD	None
Conditions and dynamics of the diverse school community	HD	SD	LD	None
Community resources	HD	SD	LD	None
Community relations and marketing strategies and processes	HD	SD	LD	None
Successful models of school, family, business, community, government and higher education partnerships	HD	SD	LD	None

Your skill/experience with processes and activities ensuring that:

High visibility, active involvement, and communication with the larger community is a priority	HD	SD	LD	None
Relationships with community leaders are identified and nurtured	HD	SD	LD	None
Information about family and community concerns, expectations, and needs issued regularly	HD	SD	LD	None
There is outreach to different business, religious, political, and service agencies and organizations	HD	SD	LD	None
Credence is given to individuals and groups whose values and opinions may conflict	HD	SD	LD	None
School and community serve one another as resources	HD	SD	LD	None
Available community resources are secured to help the schools solve problems and achieve goals	HD	SD	LD	None

Partnerships are established with area businesses, institutions of higher education, and community groups to strengthen programs and support school goals	HD	SD	LD	None
Community youth/family services are integrated with school programs	HD	SD	LD	None
Community stakeholders are treated equitably	HD	SD	LD	None
Diversity is recognized and valued	HD	SD	LD	None
Effective media relations are developed and maintained	HD	SD	LD	None
Comprehensive program of community relations is established	HD	SD	LD	None
Public resources and funds are used appropriately and wisely	HD	SD	LD	None
Community collaboration is modeled for staff	HD	SD	LD	None
Opportunities for staff to develop collaborative skills are provided	HD	SD	LD	None

ISLLC Standard 5

A school administrator is an educational leader who promotes the success of all students by *acting with integrity, fairness,* and in an *ethical manner.*
Your degree of knowledge and understanding of:

Purpose of education and the role of leadership in modern society	HD	SD	LD	None
Various ethical frameworks and perspectives on ethics	HD	SD	LD	None
Values of the diverse school community	HD	SD	LD	None
Professional codes of ethics	HD	SD	LD	None
Philosophy and history of education	HD	SD	LD	None

Your skill/experience as a leader that:

Examines personal and professional values	HD	SD	LD	None
Demonstrates a personal and professional code of ethics	HD	SD	LD	None
Demonstrates values, beliefs, and attitudes that inspire others to higher levels of performance	HD	SD	LD	None
Serves as a role model	HD	SD	LD	None
Accepts responsibility for school operations	HD	SD	LD	None
Considers the impact of one's administrative practice on others	HD	SD	LD	None
Uses the influence of the office to enhance the educational program rather than for personal gain	HD	SD	LD	None
Treats people fairly, equitably, and with dignity and respect	HD	SD	LD	None
Protects the rights and confidentiality of students and staff	HD	SD	LD	None
Demonstrates appreciation for and sensitivity to the diversity in the school community	HD	SD	LD	None
Recognizes and respects the legitimate authority of others	HD	SD	LD	None
Examines and considers the prevailing values of the diverse school community	HD	SD	LD	None
Expects that others in the school community will demonstrate integrity and exercise ethical behavior	HD	SD	LD	None
Opens the school to public scrutiny	HD	SD	LD	None
Fulfills legal and contractual obligations	HD	SD	LD	None
Applies laws & procedures fairly, wisely, and thoughtfully	HD	SD	LD	None

ISLLC Standard 6

A school administrator is an educational leader who promotes the success of all students by *understanding, responding* to, and *influencing* the larger *political, social, economic, legal,* and *cultural* context.

Your degree of knowledge and understanding of:

Principles of representative governance that are fundamental to the system of American schools	HD	SD	LD	None
The role of public education in developing and renewing a democratic society and an economically productive nation	HD	SD	LD	None
Laws relevant to education and schooling	HD	SD	LD	None
Political, social, cultural, and economic systems and processes that impact schools	HD	SD	LD	None
Models and strategies of change and conflict resolution as applied to the larger political, social, cultural, and economic contexts of schooling	HD	SD	LD	None
Global issues and forces affecting teaching and learning	HD	SD	LD	None
Dynamics of policy development and advocacy under our democratic political system	HD	SD	LD	None
Importance of diversity and equity in a democratic society	HD	SD	LD	None

Your skill/experience with processes and activities ensuring that:

The environment in which schools operate is influenced on behalf of students and their families	HD	SD	LD	None
Communication occurs within the school community concerning trends, issues, and potential changes in the environment in which schools operate	HD	SD	LD	None
There is ongoing dialogue with representatives of diverse community groups	HD	SD	LD	None
The school community works within the framework of policies, laws, and regulations enacted by local, state, and federal authorities	HD	SD	LD	None

1.3 Self, Peer, Superior, and Subordinate Assessment of ISLLC Dispositions

It's important to know yourself and know how others view you. This activity is designed to assess your dispositions in a number of areas. Some readers may be unfamiliar with the use of the term *disposition*. Disposition, in this context, describes a person's inclination to do something.

Dispositions are rooted in deeply held beliefs, values, and previous experiences. Successful leaders understand why they behave the way they do: They are aware of the beliefs and experiences that have shaped their current practice. Because successful leaders strive for a mutual understanding between themselves and those they serve, they often seek feedback from their peers, superiors, and subordinates.

An ISLLC assessment tool follows on the next page. Make copies of this assessment. Distribute a copy to a peer and a superior. You may also choose to solicit an assessment from a subordinate. Complete one copy of the evaluation yourself. Then compare the results of your self-assessment with the assessments made by others.

ISLLC Dispositions Assessment

Please circle the indicator that you believe most accurately describes evidence of the following dispositions. This is not a recommendation form on the merit or expertise of the person, but an assessment of your perspective of the beliefs behind the words and/or actions of the person. Please complete this assessment as accurately and honestly as possible. There are no good or bad, right or wrong answers—just your perceptions. Thank you for your time and effort.

SE (strong evidence); LE (limited evidence); NS (not seen); OE (opposing evidence)

Standard 1—Shared Vision

The intern believes in, values, and is committed to:

The educability of all	SE	LE	NS	OE
A school vision of high standards of learning	SE	LE	NS	OE
Continuous school improvement	SE	LE	NS	OE
The inclusion of all members of the school community	SE	LE	NS	OE

Ensuring that students have the knowledge, skills, and values needed to become successful adults	SE	LE	NS	OE
A willingness to continuously examine one's own assumptions, beliefs, and practices	SE	LE	NS	OE
Doing the work required for high levels of personal and organizational performance	SE	LE	NS	OE

Standard 2—Culture and Program for Student and Staff Growth

The intern believes in, values, and is committed to:

Student learning as the fundamental purpose of schooling	SE	LE	NS	OE
The proposition that all students can learn	SE	LE	NS	OE
The variety of ways in which students can learn	SE	LE	NS	OE
Life-long learning for self and others	SE	LE	NS	OE
Professional development as an integral part of school improvement	SE	LE	NS	OE
The benefits that diversity brings to the school community	SE	LE	NS	OE
A safe and supportive learning environment	SE	LE	NS	OE
Preparing students to be contributing members of society	SE	LE	NS	OE

Standard 3—Management and Operations

The intern believes in, values, and is committed to:

Making management decisions to enhance learning and teaching	SE	LE	NS	OE
Taking risks to improve schools	SE	LE	NS	OE
Trusting people and their judgments	SE	LE	NS	OE
Accepting responsibility	SE	LE	NS	OE

High-quality standards, expectations, and performances	SE	LE	NS	OE
Involving stakeholders in management processes	SE	LE	NS	OE
A safe environment	SE	LE	NS	OE

Standard 4—Diversity, Family, and Community

The intern believes in, values, and is committed to:

School operating as an integral part of the larger community	SE	LE	NS	OE
Collaboration and communication with families	SE	LE	NS	OE
Involvement of families and other stakeholders in school decision-making processes	SE	LE	NS	OE
The proposition that diversity enriches the school	SE	LE	NS	OE
Families as partners in the education of their children	SE	LE	NS	OE
The proposition that families have the best interests of their children in mind	SE	LE	NS	OE
Resources of the family and community needing to be brought to bear on the education of students	SE	LE	NS	OE
An informed public	SE	LE	NS	OE

Standard 5–Ethics and Integrity

The intern believes in, values, and is committed to:

The ideal of the common good	SE	LE	NS	OE
The principles of the Bill of Rights	SE	LE	NS	OE
The right of every student to a free, quality education	SE	LE	NS	OE

Bringing ethical principles to the decision-making process	SE	LE	NS	OE
Subordinating one's own interest to the good of the school community	SE	LE	NS	OE
Accepting the consequences for upholding one's principles and actions	SE	LE	NS	OE
Using the influence of one's office constructively and productively in the service of all students and their families	SE	LE	NS	OE
Development of a caring school community	SE	LE	NS	OE

Standard 6—Political, Social, Economic, Legal, and Cultural Contexts

The intern believes in, values, and is committed to:

Education as a key to opportunity and social mobility	SE	LE	NS	OE
Recognizing a variety of ideas, values, and cultures	SE	LE	NS	OE
Importance of a continuing dialogue with other decision makers affecting education	SE	LE	NS	OE
Actively participating in the political and policy-making context in the service of education	SE	LE	NS	OE
Using legal systems to protect student rights and improve student opportunities	SE	LE	NS	OE

Additional comments or elaboration on any previous items:

1.4   Other Assessments and Evaluations

The intern will gather and review other personal evaluations and assessments that are available. These will include recent annual performance evaluations, professional assessment results (e.g., NASSP assessment center, 360-degree evaluation, etc.), and other relevant assessments/evaluations completed in training, workshops, or university courses. The intern should summarize the findings and note major strengths in knowledge, skill, and experience as well as weaknesses and areas needing improvement.

1.5   Position and Leadership Goals

The intern will draft a statement of position goals and a statement of leadership goals. The position goal statement is a brief description of the desired terminal position and any positions needed or desired for advancement to that position.

The leadership goal statement addresses the purpose or motivation for leading. The statement should consider the following:

- ◆ What educational needs underlie my motivation to lead?

- ◆ What personal needs underlie my motivation to lead?

- ◆ What do I hope to accomplish as a leader?

- ◆ How will my previous accomplishments lead to school improvement?

1.6   District/School Assessment

The final assessment report must include current district/school needs. The intern should summarize and prioritize the major goals and needs for the district/school. These can be gathered from current district/school documents such as:

- ◆ District/school improvement plans

- ◆ Strategic plans

- ◆ Mission statement

- ◆ Recent accreditation reports

- ◆ Action plans

- ◆ Other evidence of district/school needs or goals.

Priorities and/or plans for the current or upcoming school year should be noted.

1.7 Assessment Summary

Following the compilation and analysis of the previously gathered information, the intern will prepare a final summary for the Overall Plan Report, which is given at the end of Stage 2. The summary should include highlights from the following:

Vita

Present a brief overview of the significant experiences and accomplishments in leadership, teaching, professional development, and service. Relevant experiences and accomplishments from other areas of the vita should also be included, that is, coaching, curriculum, graduate education, and the like, if applicable to leadership development. The intern may use a narrative or bulleted format for the presentation.

ISLLC Knowledge and Performance Self-Assessment

Include a listing of the major areas of significant knowledge and experience, as well as the major areas of limited knowledge and experience.

ISLLC Dispositions—Self, Peer, Supervisor, and Subordinate Assessments

This should include a listing of major areas of consensus for having *strong evidence* of the disposition and areas of consensus for *not seen* and/or *opposing evidence* for the disposition. The intern should also note dispositions that differ between the self-assessment and either peer, supervisor, or subordinate assessments.

Other Evaluations and/or Assessments

Include a brief summary of recent past annual performance evaluations, noting significant areas that relate to leadership and overall job performance. The intern should also provide summaries or highlights of any other evaluative or assessment data available.

Position Goal Statement and Leadership Goal Statement

Include both statements in their entirety.

District/School Needs Assessment

Include an overview of the current district/school improvement plans, strategic plans, and/or accreditation reports. This can be presented either as a narrative or in a bulleted list highlighting major goal and need areas. The intern should also note priorities for the upcoming school year.

Stage Two

Plan

Following the review of the assessment report, the intern will design the internship plan. Stage Two lists recommended or suggested activities, guidelines for service, planning a local project, and networking.

2.1 Standards, Leadership Areas, and Activities

The following standards, leadership areas, and activities are provided to assist the intern in the design of the internship. Under each standard, leadership areas essential to meeting the standard are provided. There are 38 leadership areas that the intern must include in his/her plan.

Under each leadership area are a set of suggested or recommended activities and a place to plan other activities. *It is NOT required that the intern do all of the activities listed. It IS required that the intern complete at least ONE activity for each leadership area.* The intern should choose activities that relate to previous self- and district/school assessments and goals.

It is normal for the intern plan to vary in time and effort between the leadership areas. For example, the intern may spend three hours in the area of transportation and 30 hours in scheduling or budgeting. The intent of this text is to provide the needed flexibility for the intern to address his/her individual needs, provide service to the district/school, and take advantage of present opportunities.

Listed at the end of each leadership area is the following activity:

* ☐ Other related activities approved by your supervisor, and/or service activities to district/school assigned by the supervisor, and/or activities that are part of a larger project.

Often, various needs and opportunities are present that allow for different activities than those suggested in each area. Usually, the supervising administrator will provide additional activities and seek the intern's assistance with current needs of the district/school.

Many activities use the term "district/school." The intent is for superintendent interns to observe and experience areas on a district-wide level, whereas the principalship intern will observe and experience at the school level. Interns may choose to experience one or both levels, depending on their needs and goals.

It is advisable for the intern to pencil in an "X" for the activities where he/she has a need and/or interest in gaining knowledge and skill. Following this, he/she should meet with the supervisor and collaborate on the final plan.

Vision

ISLLC Standard 1

A school administrator is an educational leader who promotes the success of all students by facilitating the development, articulation, implementation, and stewardship of a vision of learning that is shared and supported by the school community.

Skill and Experience Areas for ISLLC Standard 1: Vision

1. Vision/Mission
2. Strategic Planning
3. Data Collection and Analysis
4. Effective Communication
5. Negotiating/Consensus Building

1. *Vision/Mission*

Mark an "X" in pencil by the activity or activities you would like to include in your internship plan. You must choose at least ONE activity in this area: either one listed below or one approved by your site/university supervisor. *You are not required to undertake every suggested activity for this area.*

a. ☐ Review and compare two different district/school vision statements. Attempt to obtain these from two distinct types of districts/schools (i.e., rich/poor, urban/suburban/rural, regular/charter/private, etc.). Note strengths and weaknesses of each and make recommendations for your district/school. Include your recommendations in the notebook.

b. ☐ Review board policy on vision/mission and education plan and goals. Evaluate the degree to which congruence exists between the district/school vision/mission and goals. Interview district administrators, faculty, and staff. Obtain their views/perspectives regarding the vision/mission and education plan/goals. Assess the level of agreement among parties involved and the degree of similarity between what is stated "officially" and the actual practice in the district/school. The intern will write a reflective statement regarding how the leader would take steps to insure that the vision/mission and plans/goals drive or guide the daily practice in a district/school.

c. ☐ Review the vision statement from your district/school. Interview leaders in various departments (i.e., staff development, personnel, finance, curriculum, etc.), to assess current policy and practice that support the vision. Note policies and practices not aligned with the vision. List recommendations for greater alignment with the vision. Include your recommendations in the notebook.

d. ☐ Invite relevant constituents (i.e., students, parents, citizens), and lead this group to find consensus on the development of a district, school, or subunit vision statement. Include the final vision statement and any relevant learning from the process in the notebook.

* ☐ Other related activities approved by your supervisor, and/or service activities to district/school assigned by the supervisor, and/or activities that are part of a larger project.

2. *Strategic Planning*

Mark an "X" in pencil by the activity or activities you would like to include in your internship plan. You must choose at least ONE activity in this area: either one listed below or one approved by your site/university supervisor. *You are not required to undertake every suggested activity for this area.*

a. ☐ Review, compare, and contrast strategic plans from your district/school and another district/school. Note the goals and processes used to attain the vision. Include your comparison and recommendations in the notebook.

b. ☐ Review the strategic plan for your district/school. Note personnel involved in the plan's development, implementation, and evaluation. Investigate support and concerns from the various parties involved. Include your findings and recommendations in the notebook.

c. ☐ Serve on the strategic development, monitoring, or evaluation team for your district/school. This will depend on the current stage of the plan. Log your time and duties as part of the team. Cite significant learning and recommendations in the notebook.

d. ☐ Develop a strategic plan for your chosen project. Include the plan in the notebook.

* ☐ Other related activities approved by your supervisor, and/or service activities to district/school assigned by the supervisor, and/or activities that are part of a larger project.

3. *Data Collection and Analysis*

Mark an "X" in pencil by the activity or activities you would like to include in your internship plan. You must choose at least ONE activity in this area: either one listed below or one approved by your site/university supervisor. *You are not required to undertake every suggested activity for this area.*

a. ☐ Review board policy and administrative regulations regarding data collection, assessment, and evaluation. Evaluate the degree to which the policy and/or administrative regulations are being implemented. Write a reflective statement about ways in which the leader would seek to improve compliance in this area. If no policy/administrative regulation is in place, review other district policy/regulations in this area. The intern will prepare a policy/administrative regulation proposal for board consideration. The proposed policy/regulation will be included in notebook.

b. ☐ Review the ways in which assessment data are used by the following: board of education, superintendent, faculty, staff, and community relations/information department. Write a reflective statement about how the leader could seek to improve the use of assessment data in the district/school. The reflective statements will be included in the notebook.

*   ☐ Other related activities approved by your supervisor, and/or service activities to district/school assigned by the supervisor, and/or activities that are part of a larger project.

4. *Effective Communication*

Mark an "X" in pencil by the activity or activities you would like to include in your internship plan. You must choose at least ONE activity in this area: either one listed below or one approved by your site/university supervisor. *You are not required to undertake every suggested activity for this area.*

a. ☐ Review board policy and administrative regulations regarding how communications will be managed in the district/school. Assess the level of compliance with policy/regulations and write a reflective statement describing how you believe communications might be improved. Include the statement in the notebook.

b. ☐ Write a memo to the faculty relaying information that needs to be disseminated by the district/school office. Survey several persons receiving the memo and obtain advice on its organization, clarity, and intent and any recommendations for improvement. Include the memo and survey results in the notebook.

c. ☐ Assist in conducting a faculty meeting or staff development session. Survey a random sample of the participants for strengths and areas needing improvement from your presentation. Include the results of the survey in the notebook.

d. ☐ Choose two effective listening techniques (i.e., posing probing questions, body language, etc.), and apply the techniques in a student and/or parent conference. Personally assess the effectiveness in soliciting communication from the student and/or parent. Include assessment in the notebook.

e. ☐ Assist a current school leader in seeking information from school and community for a current project or need. Assess the various methods employed in gathering the information. Include the assessment and any recommendations in the notebook.

f. ☐ Review and critique the processes used by district/school to monitor the ongoing communication between the district/school and faculty and parents. Include your critique in the notebook.

g. ☐ In leading your selected project, gather evaluative feedback on your ability in giving information, listening, receiving information, seeking information, and monitoring information. Include the feedback in the notebook.

* ☐ Other related activities approved by your supervisor, and/or service activities to district/school assigned by the supervisor, and/or activities that are part of a larger project.

5.   *Negotiating/Consensus Building*

Mark an "X" in pencil by the activity or activities you would like to include in your internship plan. You must choose at least ONE activity in this area: either one listed below or one approved by your site/university supervisor. *You are not required to undertake every suggested activity for this area.*

a.   ☐   Review board policy and administrative regulations. Assess compliance with policy/regulations. Assess the leadership culture in the school/district. How frequent is top-down leadership versus consensus leadership used? Does the leadership style most often used comply with official policy or administrative regulation? The intern will write a reflective statement discussing the appropriate use of both top-down leadership and consensus leadership. Include the statement in the notebook.

b.   ☐   Assist in the administrative side of planning and implementing negotiations with a teacher union or teacher representative group. Note effective practices in the planning and bargaining process. Include these practices and recommendations in the notebook.

c.   ☐   Choose a current issue in the district/school. Use steps for issue resolution with a small group of concerned parties. Reach consensus for a plan to resolve the issue and/or a critique on areas where resolution failed. Include plan and critique in the notebook.

d.   ☐   In leading your selected project, include the steps you used in gaining consensus for your project plan. Include the steps and assessment of outcomes and areas for needed improvement in the notebook.

*   ☐   Other related activities approved by your supervisor, and/or service activities to district/school assigned by the supervisor, and/or activities that are part of a larger project.

Instruction and Learning

ISLLC Standard 2

A school administrator is an educational leader who promotes the success of all students by advocating, nurturing, and sustaining a school culture and instructional program conducive to student learning and staff professional growth.

Skill and Experience Areas for ISLLC Standard 2

6. Analyzing the Curriculum

7. Supervision of Instruction/
    Instructional Strategies

8. Learning/Motivation Theory

9. Learning Technology

10. Evaluation of Student Achievement/
    Testing and Measurements

11. Supervision of Extra/
    Cocurricular Education

12 Staff Development/Adult Learning

13. Change Process

14. Student Discipline

15. Student Services

6.   *Analyzing the Curriculum*

Mark an "X" in pencil by the activity or activities you would like to include in your internship plan. You must choose at least ONE activity in this area: either one listed below or one approved by your site/university supervisor. *You are not required to undertake every suggested activity for this area.*

a.   ☐   Review board policy and administrative regulations regarding curriculum development, implementation, management and evaluation/assessment. Evaluate compliance with relevant federal and state laws/mandates/regulations, and local board policy. Write a reflective statement outlining ways in which supervision/management of curriculum matters can be improved.

b.   ☐   Select one subject or course curriculum. Note the problem being addressed when it was written. Compile a list of the curriculum writers. Note which persons served as a representative for teachers, as well as the subject matter, students, learning theory, and community/state standards. Note whether any weaknesses in the curriculum are present because of lack of representation in any of these areas. Make recommendations and include them in the notebook.

c.   ☐   Interview persons involved in the implementation of a district/school curriculum. Describe the implementation process and note successes and concerns/problems with its implementation. Evaluate the process used and make recommendations for improvements and include in the notebook.

d.   ☐   The intern will take an active part in (or interview a person with experience in) the textbook selection process. The position of study should dictate the appropriate level (i.e., district, school, or department). An overview of this process, evaluative criteria used, and recommendations for improvement will be completed and included in the notebook.

e.   ☐   Evaluate the text and other reading materials for one course. Include the reading level and aspects of cultural diversity or gender bias. The evaluation and recommendations will be included in the notebook.

f.   ☐   Research the processes used for curriculum evaluation in the district/school. Evaluate the methods used, intervals of time, and degree of participation by teachers, students, and administrators. Include the evaluation and recommendations in the notebook.

g.   ☐   Go to the website of the American Psychological Association and search for "Learner-Centered Psychological Principles: A Framework" (www.apa.org/ed/lcp.html). Apply these 14 principles to understanding the strengths and weaknesses of the instructional program at your department, school, or district.

*   ☐   Other related activities approved by your supervisor, and/or service activities to district/school assigned by the supervisor, and/or activities that are part of a larger project.

7. *Supervision of Instruction/Instructional Strategies*

Mark an "X" in pencil by the activity or activities you would like to include in your internship plan. You must choose at least ONE activity in this area: either one listed below or one approved by your site/university supervisor. *You are not required to undertake every suggested activity for this area.*

a. ☐ With permission of the principal and two teachers, conduct two classroom observations using the clinical supervision model: preconference (allowing the teacher to take part in what is observed), observation, analysis, and postconference. A summary of the observation process and recommendations for improvement will be included in the notebook.

b. ☐ Following each of the classroom observations and summaries, complete the district's teacher evaluation form for the two teachers (names are NOT to be used). Note the differences between a clinical model (activity a) and the district evaluation form. The differences, recommendations, and copies of the completed forms will be included in the notebook.

c. ☐ Observe one instructional assistant. Note duties, time, and expertise in academic assistance to the students. A summary of the observation and recommendations for improvement will be included in the notebook.

d. ☐ Meet with a group of two instructional assistants and two teachers concerning the teacher evaluation process. The intern will list strengths, weaknesses, and recommendations for improvement in the process. The group should also discuss the role of the teachers and assistants in this process. A critique and recommendations of the process and role will be included in the notebook.

e. ☐ Select and administer two types of evaluation/observation instruments alternative to the official district form. Copies of the completed forms and recommendations for alternative evaluation forms will be included in the notebook.

f. ☐ Select one class to complete a student evaluation of the instruction and learning in their class. The intern will summarize the data and meet with a group of students to discuss the strengths and weaknesses of and recommendations for the process. Copies of the instrument, overview of the student meeting, and recommendations for student input in the process will be included in the notebook.

g. ☐ Interview one district-level instructional supervisor and assess current needs, goals, and level of service provided by central office instructional staff. Include the assessment and recommendations in the notebook.

* ☐ Other related activities approved by your supervisor, and/or service activities to district/school assigned by the supervisor, and/or activities that are part of a larger project.

8.   *Learning/Motivation Theory*

Mark an "X" in pencil by the activity or activities you would like to include in your internship plan. You must choose at least ONE activity in this area: either one listed below or one approved by your site/university supervisor. *You are not required to undertake every suggested activity for this area.*

a. ☐ Review methods used to encourage student motivation in the classroom. Read two articles from refereed journals on motivation strategies and discuss readings with selected administrators and faculty. Write a reflection on the topic and include in the notebook.

b. ☐ Survey a school faculty on methods used to motivate students. Survey a sample of students soliciting methods that motivate them to perform in school. Compare and contrast the two surveys. Include the comparison and recommendations in the notebook.

c. ☐ Meet with a group of similar subject-area or grade-level teachers and review the current curriculum and lesson plans. Compile the amount of traditional, behavioral, cognitive, and experiential learning objectives used. Solicit methods for utilizing more cognitive and experiential objectives in the curriculum and lesson plans. Include the compilation and recommendation in the notebook.

d. ☐ Meet with a group of teachers and assess the amount of teaching that is at each student's challenge level (Vygotsky's model). Solicit recommended methods for achieving more instruction at the differing challenge levels. Include methods and recommendations in the notebook.

e. ☐ Compile a list of all options for student groups that the district/school offers (e.g., clubs, study groups, teams). Calculate the percentage of students that belong to one or more student groups. Meet with several students, brainstorm reasons students choose not to belong, and seek recommendations for more student participation. Include the list, percentages, and recommendations in the notebook.

f. ☐   Compile a list of all examples of student recognition (e.g., honor roll, school letter jackets, most improved student awards, etc.) that the district/school practices. Calculate the percentage of students that receive some type of district/school recognition. Survey a broad spectrum of teachers, students, and parents, and elicit additional means of recognizing students.

*   ☐   Other related activities approved by your supervisor, and/or service activities to district/school assigned by the supervisor, and/or activities that are part of a larger project.

9.   *Learning Technology*

Mark an "X" in pencil by the activity or activities you would like to include in your internship plan. You must choose at least ONE activity in this area: either one listed below or one approved by your site/university supervisor. *You are not required to undertake every suggested activity for this area.*

a.   ☐   Review board policy on technology. Study district/school plan on use of technology. Review degree of compliance between policy, technology plan, and the legal aspects regarding the use of software. Include recommendations in the notebook.

b.   ☐   Using a current curriculum, gather information on present and future technology used to support teaching/learning in this subject area. The intern will make recommendations for expanded use of technology, addressing costs, training, and current and future needs of the students. Include information gathered and recommendations in the notebook.

c.   ☐   Interview persons responsible for assessing technology software. Describe the process used. Evaluate the process used, concerns, and any recommendations for improvement. Include the process description, concerns, and recommendations in the notebook.

d.   ☐   Observe the use of technology in the library and/or computer lab. Discuss the strengths and weaknesses of technology use in these areas with the librarian and/or lab supervisor and several students. Compare and contrast strengths and weakness given by the students and adults. Include the comparisons and recommendations for improvement in the notebook.

e.   ☐   Use several different search engines for finding Internet information on a particular topic. Compare the results of the searches and make recommendations for the best use for students and subject area. Include results and recommendations in the notebook.

f.   ☐   View the Draft Technology Standards for School Administrators website (http://cnets.istc.org/tssa/view_standards.html). Draw up a plan of how you will implement these six standards during your internship.

*   ☐   Other related activities approved by your supervisor, and/or service activities to district/school assigned by the supervisor, and/or activities that are part of a larger project.

10.   *Evaluation of Student Achievement/Testing and Measurements*

Mark an "X" in pencil by the activity or activities you would like to include in your internship plan. You must choose at least ONE activity in this area: either one listed below or one approved by your site/university supervisor. *You are not required to undertake every suggested activity for this area.*

a.   ☐   Review board policy and assess degree of compliance with board policy and educational plan. Discuss curriculum and assessment of student achievement with administrators and faculty. Write a reflection statement regarding the ways evaluations and assessment of student achievement might be improved. Include assessment of compliance and recommendations in notebook.

b.   ☐   Select one subject or course curriculum. Review the distribution of grades for the subject or course. Devise, distribute, and collect a brief needs assessment relating to strengths and concerns of the testing procedures and grading policy used. A copy of the assessment and recommendations for improving student performance and assessment will be included in the notebook.

c.   ☐   Gather and analyze the district/school, state, and national normed test results. Assess the current strengths and weaknesses in student achievement. Make recommendations for improvement in student performance on standardized tests. Include the assessment and recommendations in the notebook.

d.   ☐   Form and lead a team of teachers to study and develop a plan for improving test scores. The area chosen should be an area identified as a weakness in school achievement. The plan should be feasible but may require additional funds and/or a broader base of support for its implementation. Include the plan and an overview of the team process in the notebook.

e.   ☐   Randomly select a group of students and elicit their recommendations for better preparation for tests. Compile and critique the student recommendations and address the issue of student input into this process. The critique and recommendation for student input will be included in the notebook.

f.   ☐   Lead a group of common subject and/or grade-level teachers in the development and use of a six- or nine-week departmental/grade-level exam. After administering the exam, meet with the teachers and discuss the merits of this type of testing for teachers and students. Include a brief log of activities, group process used, results of your leadership, and recommendations for the use of this type of testing in the notebook.

*   ☐   Other related activities approved by your supervisor, and/or service activities to district/school assigned by the supervisor, and/or activities that are part of a larger project.

11. *Supervision of Extra-/Cocurricular Education*

Mark an "X" in pencil by the activity or activities you would like to include in your internship plan. You must choose at least ONE activity in this area: either one listed below or one approved by your site/university supervisor. *You are not required to undertake every suggested activity for this area.*

a. ☐ Review board policy and evaluate school compliance with policy in the following areas: coaches and sponsor assignments and rate of pay approved by the board on an annual basis; activities in compliance with federal law (Title IV); medical emergency plan in place and supervision plan implemented; insurance requirements complied with and evaluation of personnel and programs in place. Discuss the conduct of extracurricular activities with administration, faculty, staff, and students. Explore the perspectives of each group, and write a reflection paper with recommendations that might improve the quality of experience the district/school provides for the benefit of students.

b. ☐ Select an area of interest involving extracurricular activities. With the approval of the sponsor, assist in the planning and supervising of the activity. A critique of the learning experience for the students involved will be included in the notebook. The critique should also address student motivation, discipline, and performance, as well as their relation to the overall education of the student.

c. ☐ Collaboratively work with one staff member in the planning and supervising of a cocurricular activity. A critique of the learning experience, using the indicators listed in activity (a) will be completed and included in the notebook.

d. ☐ Meet with a group of randomly selected students to discuss the strengths and weaknesses of extra- and cocurricular activities. Recommendations for improving/expanding the strengths of such activities into other subject areas will be listed and included in the notebook.

* ☐ Other related activities approved by your supervisor, and/or service activities to district/school assigned by the supervisor, and/or activities that are part of a larger project.

12. Staff Development/Adult Learning

Mark an "X" in pencil by the activity or activities you would like to include in your internship plan. You must choose at least ONE activity in this area: either one listed below or one approved by your site/university supervisor. *You are not required to undertake every suggested activity for this area.*

a. ☐ Review board policy regarding staff development in the district/school. Discuss the role of staff development in the district/school with administrators and faculty. Assess the current staff development plan. Note the degree to which the plan provides for needed development experiences, activities, and employee input in the design. Evaluate the plan's effectiveness in the delivery of critical training required to improve staff performance. Draft a policy proposal to serve as a guide in the development of a comprehensive staff development plan. Ask respected professional educators to critique the policy proposal. Write a reflective statement on this topic, and include it in the notebook, along with the policy proposal.

b. ☐ Gather, from written evidence or from someone responsible for staff development, the yearly district/school staff development plan. The plan will be analyzed with respect to school mission, student achievement, and teacher evaluations. A copy or overview of the plan and its relationship to the above variables will be included in the notebook.

c. ☐ Collaborate with an experienced staff developer in one staff development activity. This activity should include planning, implementing, instructing, and evaluating. A copy of the agenda, relevant materials, and the evaluation will be included in the notebook.

d. ☐ Compile a list of all professional development activities completed by the faculty of a particular school. This should include activities provided by the district/school and outside of the district/school. Note discrepancies between the amount of professional development and the experience and subject areas of the teachers. Make recommendations for greater involvement in professional development by all faculty members. Include the list, patterns, and recommendations in the notebook.

e. ☐ Survey a broad spectrum of teachers to elicit recommendations for more effective and relevant professional development and to assess the degree of importance that professional development should have in teacher evaluation. Include the survey results and recommendations for effective professional development and its use in teacher evaluation.

f. ☐ Survey a broad spectrum of students to discover what they believe are the necessary areas of training for their teachers. Discuss the students' responses with the faculty and/or staff developers. Compare and contrast the perceived needs from the students with the current district/school staff development plan. Include the survey results, comparisons, and recommendations in the notebook.

* ☐ Other related activities approved by your supervisor, and/or service activities to district/school assigned by the supervisor, and/or activities that are part of a larger project.

13. *Change Process*

Mark an "X" in pencil by the activity or activities you would like to include in your internship plan. You must choose at least ONE activity in this area: either one listed below or one approved by your site/university supervisor. *You are not required to undertake every suggested activity for this area.*

a. ☐ Review board policy regarding innovations and change in the district/school. Select two or three readings from respected journals and discuss their content with faculty and administration. Assess the degree to which change theory is used to facilitate innovation and changes in district/school programs and operations. Write a reflective statement on the topic and include it in the notebook.

b. ☐ Meet with a current leader involved in implementing a district/school change. Find out why the change was made and what steps were taken to make the change. Following this, survey several persons affected by the change, and assess the support or nonsupport for the change. Analyze the stage where each person is, and recommend a means for moving the person to the next stage of change. Summarize and include in the notebook.

c. ☐ In your selected local project, devise a plan for any change affecting other individuals. Choose two of these individuals and discuss how they internalized or resisted the change. Include findings and recommendations with your project summary.

* ☐ Other related activities approved by your supervisor, and/or service activities to district/school assigned by the supervisor, and/or activities that are part of a larger project.

14. Student Discipline

Mark an "X" in pencil by the activity or activities you would like to include in your internship plan. You must choose at least ONE activity in this area: either one listed below or one approved by your site/university supervisor. *You are not required to undertake every suggested activity for this area.*

a. ☐ Review board policy and school handbooks. Review current practice in the district/school. Meet and discuss discipline with administrators in charge of student discipline, faculty, staff, students, and selected parents. Assess district/school compliance with law (state and federal), policy, regulations, and student handbooks. Write a reflective statement on student discipline and include in the notebook.

b. ☐ Examine the district/school discipline policy, and provide an analysis of its strengths and weaknesses. Include the analysis and recommendations in the notebook.

c. ☐ Review discipline referrals for a specific period, and compile the data with regard to grade level, special education classification, race, and gender. A summary of the findings and recommendations for improvement will be included in the notebook.

d. ☐ With permission of the administration, participate in a conference dealing with student discipline. Critique the session with regard to consequences imposed and the need for additional assistance with improving social skills. Include the critique and recommendations in the notebook.

e. ☐ Meet with a representative group of selected students to discuss school rules and discipline procedures. An analysis of the findings and recommendations for improvement will be included in the notebook.

f. ☐ Interview one administrator and one student who are knowledgeable about current gang behavior. An analysis of these meetings with regard to current policy and efforts in the area will be completed and included in the notebook.

* ☐ Other related activities approved by your supervisor, and/or service activities to district/school assigned by the supervisor, and/or activities that are part of a larger project.

15. Student Services

Mark an "X" in pencil by the activity or activities you would like to include in your internship plan. You must choose at least ONE activity in this area: either one listed below or one approved by your site/university supervisor. *You are not required to undertake every suggested activity for this area.*

a. ☐ Review board policy regarding student services. Assess degree of compliance with policy and education plan. Identify three ways student services might be improved and include in the notebook.

b. ☐ Participate in a career or educational program session with a counselor and a student. A critique of the session will be included in the notebook.

c. ☐ Interview a school nurse and discuss the major requirements, concerns, and goals for the school health program. Address issues such as AIDS, abuse, sex education, and any other current issues. A summary and recommendations will be included in the notebook.

d. ☐ Meet with the counselor, a member of the faculty or administration, and a parent to discuss the role of the school in regard to children responding to divorce, single parents' needs, and after-school care. Concerns and recommendations will be included in the notebook.

* ☐ Other related activities approved by your supervisor, and/or service activities to district/school assigned by the supervisor, and/or activities that are part of a larger project.

Management and Operations

ISLLC Standard 3

A school administrator is an educational leader who promotes the success of all students by ensuring management of the organization, operations, and resources for a safe, efficient, and effective learning environment.

Skill and Experience Areas for ISLLC Standard 3

16. General Office Administration

17. School Operations/Policies

18. Facility and Maintenance
    Administration/Safety and Security

19. Student Transportation

20. Food Services

21. Personnel Procedures

22. Supervision of the Budget

23. School/Program Scheduling

24. Collaborative Decision Making

16. *General Office Administration/Technology*

Mark an "X" in pencil by the activity or activities you would like to include in your internship plan. You must choose at least ONE activity in this area: either one listed below or one approved by your site/university supervisor. *You are not required to undertake every suggested activity for this area.*

a. ☐ Review the job descriptions and evaluation forms for the key office personnel at the district/school (i.e., secretary, administrative assistant, attendance officer, etc.). Following this review, meet with these persons (individually or as a group), and discuss the major duties, concerns, and recommendations for the actual work required and the relation to the job description and evaluation form.

b. ☐ Observe the office secretary for a period of time, to assess the needs and demands of his/her position. Following this observation, substitute for the administrative secretary in duties agreeable with the secretary and administration for another period of time. A brief summary of the needs and demands of this position, along with any recommendations for improvement will be included in the notebook.

c. ☐ Inventory the current administrative technology in use. This will include phone systems, computer systems, copying, fax equipment, security systems, and any other form of technology used in the administration of the district/school. The inventory will include the major uses and any major concerns with these forms of technology. The inventory and recommendations for expanded use, upgrading, or changes to current systems will be included in the notebook.

d. ☐ Review the policy and budget for administrative technology. Evaluate this policy and resources with regard to information gathered in activity (a) and other current and future needs. The evaluation and recommendations will be included in the notebook.

* ☐ Other related activities approved by your supervisor, and/or service activities to district/school assigned by the supervisor, and/or activities that are part of a larger project.

17. *School Operations/Policies*

Mark an "X" in pencil by the activity or activities you would like to include in your internship plan. You must choose at least ONE activity in this area: either one listed below or one approved by your site/university supervisor. *You are not required to undertake every suggested activity for this area.*

a. ☐ Review the policies for district/school operations. Evaluate the extent to which the district/school is in compliance with these policies. Make recommendations for increasing compliance with these policies. Include the evaluation and recommendations in the notebook.

b. ☐ Meet with the district/school attendance officer. Discuss the rules, procedures, and ramifications of attendance on law, finance, and general school/district operations. Include the highlights and/or summary of the meeting in the notebook.

c. ☐ Review the procedures for the district/school opening and closing of the school year. Observe or take an active part in these procedures. Critique the effectiveness and major concerns of these procedures. Include the critique in the notebook.

* ☐ Other related activities approved by your supervisor, and/or service activities to district/school assigned by the supervisor, and/or activities that are part of a larger project.

18.   Facility and Maintenance Administration/ Safety and Security

Mark an "X" in pencil by the activity or activities you would like to include in your internship plan. You must choose at least ONE activity in this area: either one listed below or one approved by your site/university supervisor. *You are not required to undertake every suggested activity for this area.*

a.   ☐   Examine reports from current local health and fire inspections, and any other required state or federal reporting data on maintenance of the facilities. The intern will also examine building work orders and work accomplished for the district/school. A summary of findings and recommendations will be completed and included in the notebook.

b.   ☐   Meet with the director of maintenance/head custodian and review job responsibilities and schedules of staff. Shadow/ observe one custodian and/or maintenance person for a period of time (one hour, more if possible). A brief report from the meeting and observation, including the needs, concerns, and overall assessment of work performed, will be included in the notebook.

c.   ☐   Meet with the campus/district security officer and/or building administrators and gather information on all security policies and practices. This may include metal detectors, searches, lockdowns, keys, visitor identification procedures, alarm systems, fire and emergency drills, or other practices to ensure a safe environment and manage crisis situations. Take part and/or observe as many of these practices as possible. A summary of your findings and recommendations will be included in the notebook.

*   ☐   Other related activities approved by your supervisor, and/or service activities to district/school assigned by the supervisor, and/or activities that are part of a larger project.

19. Student Transportation

Mark an "X" in pencil by the activity or activities you would like to include in your internship plan. You must choose at least ONE activity in this area: either one listed below or one approved by your site/university supervisor. *You are not required to undertake every suggested activity for this area.*

a. ☐ Interview the director of transportation and discuss the current issues and needs for transportation. This should include costs, maintenance, personnel issues, training and safety, and student problems. A brief summary of the needs and issues will be included in the notebook.

b. ☐ With the permission of the director, observe one bus driver during either a morning or afternoon bus route. A summary of observations and any recommendations will be included in the notebook.

c. ☐ Review the policies for student transportation. Evaluate the extent to which the district/school is in compliance. Be sure to consider home-to-school, school-to-home, and extra- and cocurricular procedures. Include a brief summary of the findings and recommendations in the notebook.

d. ☐ Review incident and discipline referrals occurring on the buses. Interview several students and bus drivers for concerns and recommendations for safer and more efficient bus service. Include a brief summary of the finding and recommendations in the notebook.

* ☐ Other related activities approved by your supervisor, and/or service activities to district/school assigned by the supervisor, and/or activities that are part of a larger project.

20. *Food Services*

Mark an "X" in pencil by the activity or activities you would like to include in your internship plan. You must choose at least ONE activity in this area: either one listed below or one approved by your site/university supervisor. *You are not required to undertake every suggested activity for this area.*

a. ☐ Interview the district/school food service manager and discuss the current requirements, concerns, and current issues of the program. A summary of findings from the interview will be included in the notebook.

b. ☐ Observe a food service worker in the preparation and delivery of either a breakfast or lunch meal. A summary of the observation focusing on the needs, concerns, and overall assessment of work performed will be included in the notebook.

* ☐ Other related activities approved by your supervisor, and/or service activities to district/school assigned by the supervisor, and/or activities that are part of a larger project.

21. *Personnel Procedures*

Mark an "X" in pencil by the activity or activities you would like to include in your internship plan. You must choose at least ONE activity in this area: either one listed below or one approved by your site/university supervisor. *You are not required to undertake every suggested activity for this area.*

a. ☐ Interview the person responsible for district personnel. Major requirements and issues to be discussed should include the planning, recruitment, selection, induction, compensation, evaluation, and dismissal of personnel. A summary of the interview will be included in the notebook.

b. ☐ With the permission of administration, participate in an interview for a professional position. A critique of the interviewing process will be written and included in the notebook.

c. ☐ Gather information from two or more administrators on relevant and legal questioning/assessment strategies used in the interview. Compile a list of questions to be used in hiring professional or administrators, and include it in the notebook.

d. ☐ Meet with persons responsible for personnel, and discuss the role personnel takes in planning for professional development (i.e., experience of present staff, current evaluations, future needs, etc.). Include the assessment and recommendations in the notebook.

e. ☐ Meet with administrators at the district/school level, and gather information on staff turnover (i.e., percentage, numbers in differing positions, and reasons for leaving). Gather any additional information from exit interviews. Assess the turnover rate, actions taken to address concerns, and any additional recommendations for improvement. Include assessment and recommendations in the notebook.

f. ☐ Meet with administrators at the district/school level, and gather information on placement and promotion policy and procedures. Discuss numbers of teachers teaching outside of their certification areas and the extent to which the district/school promotes and develops from within. Include a summary of the major goals, concerns, and recommendations in the notebook.

* ☐ Other related activities approved by your supervisor, and/or service activities to district/school assigned by the supervisor, and/or activities that are part of a larger project.

22. *Supervision of the Budget*

Mark an "X" in pencil by the activity or activities you would like to include in your internship plan. You must choose at least ONE activity in this area: either one listed below or one approved by your site/university supervisor. *You are not required to undertake every suggested activity for this area.*

a. ☐ Examine the school (or district) budget and the various accounts under the discretion and responsibility of the administrator of study. A brief analysis of the major functions, planning, required reporting, and major current concerns will be noted and included in the notebook.

b. ☐ Interview the administrator responsible for the district finance/budget office. The interview should focus on administrative responsibility, guidelines, training, and any other major needs or concerns that the office requires of the position of study. An overview of the interview will be included in the notebook.

c. ☐ Participate in the budget planning process for the district/school. An overview of the process and any recommendations will be included in the notebook.

d. ☐ Complete a requisition for a service or supply item from a budgeted account. A copy of the requisition and a brief description of the path it follows for approval is to be included in the notebook.

* ☐ Other related activities approved by your supervisor, and/or service activities to district/school assigned by the supervisor, and/or activities that are part of a larger project.

23. *School/Program Scheduling*

Mark an "X" in pencil by the activity or activities you would like to include in your internship plan. You must choose at least ONE activity in this area: either one listed below or one approved by your site/university supervisor. *You are not required to undertake every suggested activity for this area.*

a. ☐ Analyze the district/school schedule and make recommendations for increased efficiency and meeting student needs. Present these findings to the person responsible for scheduling to discuss their feasibility and merit. The analysis, recommendations, and comments from the person responsible for scheduling will be included in the notebook.

b. ☐ Participate in the process of student class scheduling. A brief overview of the process and any recommendations will be included in the notebook.

c. ☐ Meet with the counselor or administrator responsible for changes in student class schedules. Discuss the number of changes, rationale for changes, and ramifications of the change. Examine ways to reduce changes and/or better meet student needs. Include a summary and recommendations in the notebook.

d. ☐ Observe the opening week of school or district activities, and cite the issues and/or goals for such activities. Interview several teachers and/or students, and compare the issues and goals from their perspective. Note major concerns from administration, faculty, and students. A summary and recommendations for improvement will be included in the notebook.

e. ☐ Obtain a copy of school year closing procedures. Interview several teachers and/or students, and compare the issues and goals from their perspective. Note major concerns from administration, faculty, and students. A summary and recommendations for improvement will be included in the notebook

* ☐ Other related activities approved by your supervisor, and/or service activities to district/school assigned by the supervisor, and/or activities that are part of a larger project.

24. *Collaborative Decision Making*

Mark an "X" in pencil by the activity or activities you would like to include in your internship plan. You must choose at least ONE activity in this area: either one listed below or one approved by your site/university supervisor. *You are not required to undertake every suggested activity for this area.*

a. ☐ With permission of the superintendent/principal, observe a district cabinet, school administrative team meeting, or other meeting where the district/school leader plans to use collaborative decision making. Observe the leader's behavior in outlining goals/problem definition, seeking information, providing information, clarifying/elaborating, challenging viewpoints, diagnosing progress, and summarizing. Include the observations and recommendations for improvement in the notebook.

b. ☐ In any of the activities chosen where you will be leading a group, practice each of the group leadership tasks cited in the above activity (a). At the conclusion of the meeting, have the group members complete an evaluation of your performance of each of the tasks. Include a summary of the evaluations and recommendations for improvement in the notebook.

c. ☐ Survey district administrators or school teachers to assess how they wish to participate in collaborative decision making. Include in the survey their perceived level of interest and expertise, as well as the need for a high-quality decision and support for the decision. Discuss the results of the survey with the superintendent or principal, and compare agreement or disagreement with the administrators' and teachers' desires and their beliefs and practices. Include a summary and recommendations in the notebook.

*   ☐ Other related activities approved by your supervisor, and/or service activities to district/school assigned by the supervisor, and/or activities that are part of a larger project.

Community

ISLLC Standard 4

A school administrator is an educational leader who promotes the success of all students by collaborating with families and community members, responding to diverse community interests and needs, and mobilizing community resources.

Skill and Experience Areas for ISLLC Standard 4

25. Community/Public Relations
26. Parent Involvement
27. Climate for Cultural Diversity
28. Community/Business Involvement and Partnerships

25. *Community/Public Relations*

Mark an "X" in pencil by the activity or activities you would like to include in your internship plan. You must choose at least ONE activity in this area: either one listed below or one approved by your site/university supervisor. *You are not required to undertake every suggested activity for this area.*

a. ☐ Interview one or more persons involved in district/school public relations. The interview should include strategies for effective communication to and from the community and the issue of community politics. A summary of the interview will be included in the notebook.

b. ☐ With the person from activity (a) or another in the department, assist in the preparation of a written communication to be sent out to the public. A copy of the communication will be included in the notebook.

c. ☐ Investigate through knowledgeable persons in the district to ascertain who are the leading groups and individuals in the community. Using brief phone interviews, discuss their assessment of communication with the district/school, issues and concerns, and recommendations for improved relations. Include a summary and recommendations in the notebook.

d. ☐ Using the summary and recommendations for (c), meet with one board member or district/school administrator, and compare their perspective and plans for improved community relations. Include a summary and recommendations in the notebook.

* ☐ Other related activities approved by your supervisor, and/or service activities to district/school assigned by the supervisor, and/or activities that are part of a larger project.

26. *Parent Involvement*

Mark an "X" in pencil by the activity or activities you would like to include in your internship plan. You must choose at least ONE activity in this area: either one listed below or one approved by your site/university supervisor. *You are not required to undertake every suggested activity for this area.*

a.   ☐   Develop a general questionnaire addressing school policy, instruction, homework, activities, discipline, and parent involvement. Distribute the questionnaire to a group of parents. A summary of the findings concerning parent attitudes about school will be included in the notebook.

b.   ☐   Examine the current policy and procedures for parent involvement in the school/district. A brief summary of the district's or school's initiatives in parent involvement will be included in the notebook.

c.   ☐   Write a short proposal for increasing or improving parent involvement and attitude toward the school. The proposal will be included in the notebook.

d.   ☐   Observe a meeting of the site-based council. The intern will assess the role of the parents in the process, and provide recommendations for increasing the effectiveness of their role. The agenda, outcomes of the meeting, and recommendations will be included in the notebook.

*   ☐   Other related activities approved by your supervisor, and/or service activities to district/school assigned by the supervisor, and/or activities that are part of a larger project.

27. *Climate for Cultural Diversity*

Mark an "X" in pencil by the activity or activities you would like to include in your internship plan. You must choose at least ONE activity in this area: either one listed below or one approved by your site/university supervisor. *You are not required to undertake every suggested activity for this area.*

a. ☐ Examine and evaluate the school library with regard to resources that address the heritage and values of a culturally diverse and/or bilingual population. A copy of the evaluation will be included in the notebook.

b. ☐ Meet with members of the language arts and/or reading departments, and examine the literature used with regard to gender stereotyping. An analysis and recommendations will be included in the notebook.

c. ☐ Develop and implement a plan to promote cultural diversity in the district, school, or classroom. A copy of the plan will be included in the notebook.

d. ☐ Meet confidentially with one or more students of differing racial groups to assess their concerns and recommendations for a positive culturally diverse climate in the district/school. A summary and critique of the interview will be included in the notebook.

e. ☐ Meet confidentially with one or more parents of differing racial groups to assess their concerns and recommendations for a positive culturally diverse climate in the district/school. A summary and critique of the interview will be included in the notebook.

* ☐ Other related activities approved by your supervisor, and/or service activities to district/school assigned by the supervisor, and/or activities that are part of a larger project.

28. *Community/Business Involvement and Partnerships*

Mark an "X" in pencil by the activity or activities you would like to include in your internship plan. You must choose at least ONE activity in this area: either one listed below or one approved by your site/university supervisor. *You are not required to undertake every suggested activity for this area.*

a. ☐ Compile a list of social agencies that are available to help and support the district/school students, faculty, and administration. The list of agencies and their major services provided will be included in the notebook.

b. ☐ Interview one social service worker (identified in activity a) who provides assistance to students or faculty. The interview will focus on the needs of the clients served and the worker's view of the role of the school in meeting these needs. A summary of the interview and any recommendations for improvement will be included in the notebook.

c. ☐ Interview two business/community leaders that reside in the district/school attendance zone. The interview will focus on their perceptions of the quality of education, concerns, and recommendations for the schools. A summary of the interview will be included in the notebook.

d. ☐ Gather information on the resources available to the schools from community and business. The intern will analyze the extent of utilization, make recommendations for improved cooperation and mutual benefit, and include these in the notebook.

e. ☐ Attend a school meeting where one of the key community or business organizations that cooperate with the district/school is in attendance. A brief summary of the meeting and its relevance to the school will be included in the notebook.

* ☐ Other related activities approved by your supervisor, and/or service activities to district/school assigned by the supervisor, and/or activities that are part of a larger project.

Ethics

ISLLC Standard 5

A school administrator is an educational leader who promotes the success of all students by acting with integrity and fairness and in an ethical manner.

Skill and Experience Areas for ISLLC Standard 5

29. Position Goals and Requirements

30. Philosophy/History of Education

31. Ethics

32. Interpersonal Relationships

29. *Position Goals and Requirements*

Mark an "X" in pencil by the activity or activities you would like to include in your internship plan. You must choose at least ONE activity in this area: either one listed below or one approved by your site/university supervisor. *You are not required to undertake every suggested activity for this area.*

a. ☐ Obtain a copy of the job description and evaluation instrument used for the position of study. Analyze the correlation between the requirements listed in the job description and the performance standards of the evaluation. Copies of job description and evaluation and the analysis will be included in notebook.

b. ☐ Review the above materials, and interview one supervisor responsible for evaluation of the position of study. Determine the degree of subjectivity in the evaluation process and any additional criteria used in determining the final evaluation. A summary of the interview should be included in the notebook.

c. ☐ Gather and compile a list of current demands/goals that are being placed under the responsibility of the position of study. These may come from a state or board mandate, a strategic plan, a campus improvement plan, or community concerns. Relate these goals to areas on the job description and evaluation. The list of demands/goals and their relation to job description and evaluation are to be included in the notebook.

* ☐ Other related activities approved by your supervisor, and/or service activities to district/school assigned by the supervisor, and/or activities that are part of a larger project.

30. Philosophy/History of Education

Mark an "X" in pencil by the activity or activities you would like to include in your internship plan. You must choose at least ONE activity in this area: either one listed below or one approved by your site/university supervisor. *You are not required to undertake every suggested activity for this area.*

a.   ☐   Find a retired/elderly educator, and conduct an interview. Focus on the oral history of the community and school system. Note significant events that affect the district/school today. Include highlights of the interview in the notebook.

b.   ☐   Write a story about the person you met in activity (a). Include biography, education, and his or her philosophy of practice. How do these connect?

c.   ☐   Review past school board agendas, reports, and/or minutes. Note significant events, policy changes, and recurring themes or concerns that impact the district/school today. Include a summary in the notebook.

d.   ☐   Review the officially adopted curriculum in one area. Note the philosophical base that underlies the curriculum. Cite any recommendations for inclusion of other philosophies that would better serve the needs of all students. Include your recommendations in the notebook.

e.   ☐   In a planned project that you lead, cite any relevant historical background. List one or more significant educational philosophers that would support the project goal. This information will be included in the background section of the project report.

*   ☐   Other related activities approved by your supervisor, and/or service activities to district/school assigned by the supervisor, and/or activities that are part of a larger project.

31. *Ethics*

Mark an "X" in pencil by the activity or activities you would like to include in your internship plan. You must choose at least ONE activity in this area: either one listed below or one approved by your site/university supervisor. *You are not required to undertake every suggested activity for this area.*

a. ☐ Draft a list of the guiding principles for ethical behavior that you currently employ. Interview one school and one business/civic leader, and solicit the principles that they employ. Compare and contrast the lists. Include the lists, comparisons, and recommendations in the notebook.

b. ☐ Meet with a group of school staff members (i.e., secretaries, clerks, etc.), and discuss their perspectives of ethical/unethical behaviors employed by the certified personnel in the district/school. Seek recommendations for policy changes, additional training, and/or consequences to ensure increased ethical practices by certified personnel. Include recommendations in notebook.

c. ☐ Meet with a representative group of students. Solicit their beliefs and experiences with ethical practices in the school/classroom. Using the student perspectives, make recommendations for ensuring greater ethical practices for all students and include in the notebook.

d. ☐ Following the completion of your local project, obtain evaluative feedback on the ethical practices that you used in leading the project. Include feedback and any recommendations in the notebook.

e. ☐ Provide evidence that you actually do what you tell others to do. For example, if you ask others to monitor and adjust their performances, show how you do this in your work.

* ☐ Other related activities approved by your supervisor, and/or service activities to district/school assigned by the supervisor, and/or activities that are part of a larger project.

32. *Interpersonal Relationships*

Mark an "X" in pencil by the activity or activities you would like to include in your internship development plan. You must choose at least ONE activity in this area: either one listed below or one approved by your site/university supervisor. *You are not required to undertake every suggested activity for this area.*

a. ☐ Choose from the following list of interpersonal skills the ones you wish to focus on and develop throughout the school year. It is recommended that you first choose two to four, but you may add others as you become proficient in your first choices.

- Converses with others in a positive and pleasant manner
- Avoids criticizing and values diverse opinions/perspectives
- Avoids interrupting others while speaking
- Acknowledges accomplishments of others
- Promptly gets back to others with concerns or needs
- Shares information with others that need to know
- Accepts criticism
- Avoids being defensive when challenged
- Shares self with others
- Seeks to know and understand others

When leading meetings:
- Encourages others to participate
- Acknowledges feelings and mood relationships within the group
- Eases tensions when they occur
- Attempts to resolve conflicts constructively
- Encourages consideration of varying perspectives
- Empathetic to others
- Shares responsibilities

* ☐ Other related activities approved by your supervisor, and/or service activities to district/school assigned by the supervisor, and/or activities that are part of a larger project.

Political, Social, Legal, Economic, and Cultural Context

ISLLC Standard 6

A school administrator is an educational leader who promotes the success of all students by understanding, responding to, and influencing the larger political, social, economic, legal, and cultural context.

Areas for ISLLC Standard 6

33. School Board Policy and Procedures/
    State and Federal Law

34. Federal Programs Administration

35. Issue and Conflict Resolution

36. Current Issues Affecting Teaching
    and Learning

37. Professional Affiliations and Resources

38. Professional Library

33. *School Board Policy and Procedures/ State and Federal Law*

Mark an "X" in pencil by the activity or activities you would like to include in your internship plan. You must choose at least ONE activity in this area: either one listed below or one approved by your site/university supervisor. *You are not required to undertake every suggested activity for this area.*

a. ☐ Attend as many board meetings as possible. Include the agendas in notebook, followed by a list of outcomes/decisions pertaining to each agenda item.

b. ☐ Review the board policy manual. Next, interview the superintendent or assistant superintendent to discuss the compilation and updating process of the manual and the role of the board in this process. A summary of the interview will be included in the notebook.

c. ☐ Review the board training requirements and the role of the superintendent in this process. A summary of requirements, process, and the superintendent's role will be included in the notebook.

d. ☐ Interview a board member or central office person experienced in the school bond process. Information gathered should include planning, public relations, and legal requirements. A summary of this interview should be included in the notebook.

e. ☐ Interview a board member to discuss establishing positive relations with the superintendent. The intern will interview the superintendent and also discuss relations with the board. A critique covering the similarities and differences between these perspectives will be included in the notebook.

* ☐ Other related activities approved by your supervisor, and/or service activities to district/school assigned by the supervisor, and/or activities that are part of a larger project.

34. *Federal Programs Administration*

Mark an "X" in pencil by the activity or activities you would like to include in your internship plan. You must choose at least ONE activity in this area: either one listed below or one approved by your site/university supervisor. *You are not required to undertake every suggested activity for this area.*

a.   Attend one special education meeting involving initial placement or annual review. A critique of the meeting will be included in the notebook.

b.   Interview a professional responsible for vocational education. Major requirements, concerns, and goals for the program will be discussed. Summarize these issues, and cite current and future plans to address these issues. The summary will be included in the notebook with recommendations for improvement.

c.   Interview a professional responsible for the bilingual and/or ESL program. Major requirements, concerns, and goals for the program should be discussed. Then observe a bilingual or ESL class and following the observation, discuss these issues with the teacher. A summary of the interview, observation, and discussion will be written and included in the notebook.

d.   Interview professionals responsible for the title/chapter program, gifted education, and at-risk program. Current issues and goals should be discussed and a summary included in the notebook.

e.   Interview one professional with experience in writing grants. Review one such grant, and highlight the requirements and procedures for writing and submitting the grant and include this in the notebook.

*   Other related activities approved by your supervisor, and/or service activities to district/school assigned by the supervisor, and/or activities that are part of a larger project.

35. *Issue and Conflict Resolution*

Mark an "X" in pencil by the activity or activities you would like to include in your internship plan. You must choose at least ONE activity in this area: either one listed below or one approved by your site/university supervisor. *You are not required to undertake every suggested activity for this area.*

a.   ☐   Choose a current issue at your district/school. Find at least two persons on either side of the issue. Meet with the chosen persons in a group or individually to ascertain the goals for each side. Ensure each side understands the goals of the other side. Develop a list of concerns that each side believes about the opposing side. Devise a resolution that helps both sides achieve their goals and addresses all concerns. Meet with both sides to reach consensus on the new proposal or plan. Include the goals, list of concerns, and consensus on goals in the notebook. Include any recommendations for the school/district concerning the issue.

*   ☐   Other related activities approved by your supervisor, and/or service activities to district/school assigned by the supervisor, and/or activities that are part of a larger project.

36. *Current Issues Affecting Teaching and Learning*

Mark an "X" in pencil by the activity or activities you would like to include in your internship plan. You must choose at least ONE activity in this area: either one listed below or one approved by your site/university supervisor. *You are not required to undertake every suggested activity for this area.*

a.   Compile a list of current issues that affect teaching and learning. Use research literature and perspectives from administrators, teachers, students, and parents in compiling the list. Assess the degree of importance and urgency for each issue. Include your list and assessment with any recommendations in your notebook.

*   Other related activities approved by your supervisor, and/or service activities to district/school assigned by the supervisor, and/or activities that are part of a larger project.

37. *Professional Affiliations and Resources*

Mark an "X" in pencil by the activity or activities you would like to include in your internship plan. You must choose at least ONE activity in this area: either one listed below or one approved by your site/university supervisor. *You are not required to undertake every suggested activity for this area.*

a. ☐ Contact several persons experienced in the position of study, and compile a list of professional associations; service organizations; and local, state, and federal agencies that provide expertise and service to the position. The list of resources and their major area of service are to be included in the notebook.

b. ☐ Submit a brief professional development plan. Plans should include deficiencies cited in the internship in the various learning areas. The plan should also include ongoing development with membership and service to pertinent organizations cited in the above activity. The professional development plan is to be included in the notebook.

*   ☐ Other related activities approved by your supervisor, and/or service activities to district/school assigned by the supervisor, and/or activities that are part of a larger project.

38. *Professional Library*

Mark an "X" in pencil by the activity or activities you would like to include in your internship plan. You must choose at least ONE activity in this area: either one listed below or one approved by your site/university supervisor. *You are not required to undertake every suggested activity for this area.*

a.   Compile a list of books, publications, training manuals, and district or state publications used or recommended for the position in question. The list should include resources of the highest quality and relevance to the position and educational leadership. The list should be included in the notebook.

*   Other related activities approved by your supervisor, and/or service activities to district/school assigned by the supervisor, and/or activities that are part of a larger project.

2.2 Meeting with Site Supervisor

After completing Stage 1 and making preliminary choices of activities in the 38 skill and experience areas, the intern should meet with the site supervisor to reach consensus on a plan for the internship. The intern and site supervisor should discuss the intern's preferred activities and decide the nature of the service activities and the local project described in Sections 2.3 and 2.4.

2.3 Service Activities

Education is a service profession. The intern should plan for appropriate modeling and accomplishments of service. The internship must balance the needs of the intern and the needs of the district/school.

Care must be taken, however, that a realistic balance between intern need and school need is maintained. The final plan should not be centered selfishly on your development, nor should you limit your experience by submitting totally to the specific needs or concerns of the district/school.

Service activities will come mainly from the site supervisor's recommendations. They will be written in the "other" category listed under each of the 36 leadership areas. These may be assistance on current needs and projects, assistance with day-to-day administrative duties, or any other needs that the site-supervisor believes will benefit the district/school and the intern.

2.4 Local Project

The intern is required to conduct at least one local project. The project should be directly related to the district/school goals. The project must:

- ◆ Include other faculty or staff in a group process
- ◆ Be led by the intern
- ◆ Have a plan that includes:
  - • Need for the project
  - • Goal of the project
  - • Resources available
  - • Timeline
  - • Method of evaluation
- ◆ Include other experience and skill areas (e.g., decision making, communication, etc.)
- ◆ Be approved by the supervisor

The intern may choose a large project or several smaller projects. It is strongly recommended that the size and number of projects be considered with respect to time needed to fulfill other activities and current job responsibilities.

2.5 Networking

All leaders use networks to seek advice, discuss ideas, and improve their ability to fulfill the responsibilities of their positions. These networks often consist of mentors, peers, and experts in various fields. Contacts may also include community leaders, colleagues from professional organizations, and the like.

The intern should keep a directory of key personnel used and any additional persons that he or she discovers during the internship. After choosing skill and experience activities, service activities, and local project(s), the intern should cite key persons that he or she plans to work with, interview, and/or use for help and assistance with his/her internship. Resource persons should give their permission, means of communication (phone, e-mail, or times available). Some interns find it more efficient to collect and maintain a file of business cards. The documented resource network will be presented at the final internship summary report.

2.6 Organizing a Notebook

The intern is required to obtain and use a notebook. Typically the notebook is a large, three-ring binder with sections devoted to the 38 activity areas. The intern may add other documents for the internship in the notebook, such as the list of networking contacts, log, evaluations, and summaries. Documents collected in the notebook may be used to develop the intern's professional portfolio.

2.7 Internship Overall Plan Report

In this activity, the intern will prepare and present an overall plan report. Typically, the intern will present this to his/her supervisors, either as part of many reports by others or by itself. The report must be a professional presentation, similar to reporting to the board. Documentation should include:

+ Activities planned from the 38 leadership areas
+ Service activities
+ Overall plan for the local project(s)
+ List of resource persons to be used
+ Estimated hours for the internship
+ Estimated completion date

Stage Three

Implementation

3.1 Interviewing

It is highly recommended that the intern plan to schedule interviews with various school and community leaders. Interviews, however, should be only a small part of the overall experience. The vast majority of time should be spent working as opposed to observing or listening. Interviewing can affect several key outcomes that the intern should consider. These include:

- Meeting the right people/developing a network of experienced school leaders

- Knowing the various leadership positions and their responsibilities

- Providing the opportunity for current leaders to get to know you

- Forming new relationships—administrator to intern administrator, versus administrator to teacher/other

- Understanding different departments and perceptions from leaders/followers within each department

- Getting the "bigger picture" and having experienced mentors provide answers to questions/concerns from various areas and perspectives

- Interview questions:

- Tell me about your department/area.

- Tell me about your job duties and responsibilities.

- What are your goals?

- What are your present major concerns?

- What future concerns are anticipated?

- What do you need, expect, or hope for from your principal or superintendent?

- ♦ From your experience of working with your district/school, what advice would you give a new principal or superintendent?

- ♦ What activities would you suggest I undertake during my internship to better understand and/or work with your department/area?

Add any additional questions appropriate to your knowledge, experience, or project.

3.2 Theory Into Practice: Using the 10 Major Skills

Although Kurt Lewin was right to say, "There is nothing so practical as good theory," it is equally true that there is nothing so theoretical as good practice (Fullan, 2001). Wise leaders do not subscribe to the notion of universal truths in educational administration and realize the need to analyze the beliefs, traditions, and experiences that form their theories of reality and guide their practice. Hoy and Miskel (2001) conclude that theory relates to practice in three ways: Theory forms a frame of reference for the practitioner, theorizing provides for a general mode of analysis of practical events, and theory guides decision making.

This section provides a brief overview of the 10 major skills for leadership development. It is intended to provide a frame of reference for the intern for reflection, practice, and assessment of development. It is assumed that the intern has previous instruction and more in-depth study in each of these areas:

1. Vision
2. Decision Making
3. Communication
4. Conflict and Issue Resolution
5. Motivation
6. Group Processes
7. Leadership Style and Power
8. Culture and Climate
9. Change
10. Evaluation

Following the overviews of the 10 major skills, a list of questions for each of the areas is provided. Use these for analysis of current performance and the development of future actions (decisions) to address the current problem and assist in alleviating future similar problems.

When problems occur or needs arise, people tend to focus on the immediate crisis. This focus may alleviate the current need, but it does little to ensure that organizational learning has occurred or similar problems will occur less often. In these situations, leaders find themselves endlessly putting out the same types of fires. Consideration of each of the 10 areas gives the leader the big picture and the necessary information to guide future actions for organizational improvement and a heightened quality of life within the organization. To gather the necessary information, the leader has to ask the right questions. These analysis questions provide for a more comprehensive definition of the problem and thus allow for more appropriate actions.

A sample case is given in Appendix A.7. In this textbook case, the questions from the 10 areas are used for analysis and generation of future actions. It is recommended that the intern review the case and note the breadth and depth of analysis it provides. Further practice on textbook cases will assist in forming the proper mental framework for viewing problems or needs. With enough practice, this framework of thinking becomes almost second nature to the leader. For optimal learning, it is advised that the intern use real-life cases and cooperative learning groups. Great learning occurs with the practice of analysis and consideration of a variety of perspectives.

1. Vision

Of the popularly expressed requirements for leadership, one of the most common is that leaders have vision (Gardner, 1990). Vision is one aspect research has long held that separates leaders from administrators or managers. The administrative manager is one that "copes with complexity" or manages the current status quo, whereas the leader is "coping with" and initiating change (Lipham, 1964; Kotter, 1998). Thus managers are concerned with the efficiency of the current system, whereas leaders look for greater effectiveness with new policies, procedures, and systems.

It is difficult to lead in schools today with many teachers and parents fearful of and resistant to change. It is equally difficult to lead the district or school when only those elected have the power to change. In addition, beginning school administrators attempt to do things right and fulfill their job descriptions; they begin to behave like managers, not leaders. Realize that your vision involves risk and few administrators are risk takers in their early years of administration.

Reducing risk and increasing the possibility of success for your vision require all the other nine skills. It takes good decisions, effective communication, resolving conflict, effective motivation strategies, groups working together, proper style and use of power, a positive culture and safe climate, understanding change, and effective evaluation strategies. The central ingredient for the realization of the vision is trust (Bennis & Nanus, 1985). Trust in the leader, trust in the followers, and trust in the vision can be developed only through the *shared* work in all areas.

Leaders strive to move the organization and all of its members to a new vision. The vision and the means to get there require understanding, effort, and support from the entire organization. Leaders do not have to create the vision by themselves, but they are responsible for providing the leadership for vision creation, articulation, and support.

Analysis Questions for Vision

- ◆ Is there a clear vision of how the organization should be functioning now and in the future? Is it shared by all?

- ◆ Is the mission of the organization appropriate, understood, and supported?

- ◆ Has adequate planning been done?

- ◆ Are the vision, mission, and plans aligned with the key principles and beliefs of those in the organization?

- ◆ Has trust been established among leadership, faculty, students, and community?

- ◆ What actions need to be taken to address any of the above concerns to solve the current problem and avoid similar problems in the future?

Future school leaders must utilize research, practice, reflect, and form habits of developing and working toward the realization of the vision.

2. Decision Making

Decision making is sine qua non to educational administration because the school, like all formal organizations, is basically a decision-making structure (Hoy and Miskel, 2001).

Decision making is a process that guides actions. Decisions are based on one's beliefs, values, and previous experiences. Leaders must know themselves, know why they choose particular paths, know whom to involve, and know which particular decision-making model to use.

It is assumed that interns have deliberated on their key beliefs and principles and have some degree of understanding of the similarities and differences between themselves and others. They should continue to use reflection to make decisions: Reflection will help interns more fully understand the roots of their beliefs and the impact of those beliefs on decisions. This section will briefly review levels of involvement and the major decision-making models.

Educational leadership has come a long way since the scientific management era in the early twentieth century. Then, the ones at the top made the decisions and believed that a rational model would shape optimal decisions. They believed they could actually know all alternatives and predict the results of each alternative. Today, we know better. We know that those at the top cannot accurately gather or predict all alternatives. We know that followers deserve to be involved and better decisions are made with input and collaboration. The first decision is to decide what level of involvement is most effective.

Leaders have at least four options of involvement in decisions: *deciding alone, seeking participation and input, seeking collaboration,* and *letting others decide.* These approaches are termed *autocratic, participative, collaborative,* and *laissez faire,* respectively. The wise leader uses participative and collaborative strategies for all-important decisions. However, this cannot always be done, nor should it always be done. The leader must assess five factors to decide on the level of involvement:

1. *Time.* Urgency may require the leader to decide him/herself. Participative decisions, especially collaboration, require more time than a decision made alone. If important decisions are at stake, the leader must schedule more time for involvement.

2. *Staff interest in the decision.* Barnard (1938) found that individuals have a "zone of indifference," where they simply accept the leader's decision and are apathetic toward the decision. In these cases, the leader would not benefit from trying to gain participation or collaboration. At higher levels of interest, however, it is appropriate for more participation or collaboration. For leaders desiring more collaboration, interest in the decision must first be generated.

3. *Expertise of the staff.* At very low levels of expertise, followers accept the decisions of the leader. Higher levels of expertise require either participation or collaboration for a successful decision. Again, the leader who wants collaboration must raise levels of expertise to successfully involve subordinates.

4. *Importance or need for a high-quality decision.* Some decisions are much more important and carry significant consequences. Imagine that you must decide whether to organize staff mailboxes by department or in alphabetical order. Now imagine that you must decide which teacher will be hired from a pool of candidates. Which decision will have more impact? For important questions that demand a high-quality decision, collaboration is the best model. If the deci-

sion is relatively unimportant, then the leader should simply make the decision.

5. *Degree of need for buy-in and support for the decision.* Many decisions in schools need the support of the staff for successful implementation and results. A collaborative model often increases buy-in and support.

We live in a time of empowerment and involvement in decisions. The wise leader understands that better decisions are made with higher levels of involvement. This leader also understands that involvement does not simply happen and is not always the best approach. Greater involvement and a collaborative (shared) decision model take time to plan, and it takes effort to educate and motivate staff to participate effectively. The resulting better decisions are worth the effort.

A laissez-faire model is seldom recommended. There are situations, however, where the leader has little interest or expertise, while others on the staff do. In these rare instances, this model may be appropriate.

The effective school leader should know and be able to use a variety of decision models. The five models most often seen in research are *classical, satisficing, incremental, mixed scanning,* and *garbage can.*

1. The *classical* (also known as *rational* or scientific) model strives for the single best decision. It uses the traditional steps of defining the problem, gathering information, listing alternatives, predicting outcomes, deciding on the best alternative, implementing, and evaluating. As stated earlier, this sounds correct in theory, but it is difficult to implement in real life (which operates with a host of unknown future events).

2. Herbert Simon (1947) examined the way administrators really made decisions. He found that leaders did not seek the best decision but a satisfactory one. If the leader can find an alternative that satisfies the followers, then that is the decision to make. The use of this model, called the *satisficing* model, is situational. If the followers are highly expert and experienced, then the potential for a successful decision is high. If the others have little expertise or experience, the potential for a successful decision is limited.

3. Charles Lindblom (1959) introduced the third decision model. This model is called *incremental* (or muddling through). This option is used when the leader does not know the best solution or even any satisfactory alternative. In this circumstance, the leader takes steps similar to his/her current practice to see if improvement occurs. The main concern with this model is that the steps may or may not be

aligned with the philosophy or mission and thus may move in the wrong direction.

4. Amitai Etzioni (1967) introduced what he believed was a union between rational and muddling through. This adaptive strategy, called *mixed scanning*, allows the leader to take steps but ensures that the steps are aligned and assist in reaching the mission of the organization. In situations with incomplete information and inadequate time, this model provides the leader with the additional time and offers a possibility of finding a satisfactory decision.

5. Cohen, March, and Olsen (1972) originated the *garbage can* model. Although seldom used, it is a model that acts before problem definition. In some situations, leaders want to implement something that they have utilized previously. They "remove it from the garbage can" and decide to implement. Obviously, considering the model's failure to adapt to the new circumstances, new personnel, and new students, it has a high potential for failure. Although not recommended, the originators found that it was a strategy that many administrators used.

Analysis Questions for Decision Making

- ♦ Is there a need for the decision?
- ♦ Were the major steps in decision making followed?
  - Definition of the problem and gathering information
  - Identification of alternatives
  - Assessment of alternatives
  - Selection of best alternative
  - Acceptance/support of decision
  - Implementation of decision
  - Evaluation of decision
- ♦ Was the appropriate decision-making model used?
  - Rational/scientific (classical)—use of major steps to find one best solution; used for narrow, simple problems with complete information and certain outcomes
  - Satisficing—use of major steps to find consensus (all satisfied) on solution; used with complex problems with partial information, uncertainty, but with definable satisfactory outcomes and adequate time for deliberation

- Incremental—choosing several alternatives and comparing results until agreement on course of action; used with incomplete information, complex problems, outcomes uncertain, no guiding policy, and general organizational chaos

- Mixed scanning—same as incremental, but alternatives must be aligned with mission and philosophy; used with incomplete information, complex problems, uncertain outcomes, but a guiding policy and mission

- Garbage can—use of a previous solution to fit the current problem or no problem; used when dissatisfaction is present and solution is attractive

♦ Was the appropriate level of involvement used?

♦ Were those affected by the decision included in the process?

♦ What actions need to be taken to address any concerns from above to solve the current problem and avoid similar problems in the future?

Future school leaders must utilize research, practice, reflect, and form habits of choosing the appropriate decision-making model and level of involvement.

3. Communication

In the area of leadership, there is no skill more essential than communication (Guarino, 1974). Without exception, all major national school administration associations in this country stress the importance of effective communication skills (Gorton & Snowden, 2002). Despite these findings, schools are generally criticized for poor communication between leaders and faculty, teachers and other teachers, faculty and students, and school and community. Future school leaders must utilize research, practice, reflect, and form habits of effective communication.

What do we know about communication? First, it is impossible for one person to imagine a concept or event, find the words or actions to describe (encode) it, relay these words or actions (transmit), and make another person understand (decode) the message exactly the way it was originally imagined. The difficulty of transmitting the feelings, impressions, and related experience unique to every individual only magnifies this dilemma. It is the leader's responsibility to continuously work toward more effective communication and better understanding among all individuals.

Second, we know that there are four major communication skill areas. The first is that leaders must be proficient in giving information. This includes oral, written, and technological information (e-mail, web pages, Excel, Power Point, etc). Leaders must develop effective two-way communication. They must also be highly proficient in the second area of communication: listening and receiving information. These two aspects of communication involve verbal and nonverbal strategies and cues. The five strongest nonverbal influences are smiling, touching, affirmative head nods, immediacy behavior (leaning forward, facing the individual), and eye behavior (Heintzman et al., 1993). The successful leader develops both effective verbal and nonverbal behaviors.

In considering both giving and receiving information, a leader should emphasize receiving information. Covey (1989) found that successful leaders seek to understand before they seek to be understood. Listening and receiving information first allow the leader to have the whole picture, as opposed to giving information and allowing only others to know both sides and perspectives. Carnegie (1993) teaches that no one is more persuasive than a good listener. Listening results in many other positive outcomes. These include:

- Showing interest and respect for others

- Allowing others to vent

- Increasing your learning and understanding

- Providing for resolution of conflict

- Forming the habit and appearance of wisdom

- Modeling an appropriate social skill

- Allowing extra time for observing others' communication styles, for example, body language, inflection, emotion, etc.

- Allowing extra time for listening to what your mind, heart, emotion, and body are telling you

- Building rapport and meaningful relationships

- Developing a culture of open communication

The third aspect of effective communication is the design and management of a communication system. Ultimately, the leader is responsible for communications within the organization and outside the organization. Without an effective system, the leader must depend on others for the accuracy and amount of information. This is often less than adequate because:

- Others often tell leaders only what they believe the leader wants to hear

- Others may tell the leader only the positive side

- Others may tell the leader only the negative side

- Others often omit vital information

- Many do not communicate with the leader

An effective communication system involves a variety of formats and avenues of communication. Successful leaders may regularly use meetings, surveys, interviews, group processes, suggestion boxes, needs assessments, open-door policies, the practice of walking the halls and eating in the cafeteria, and a host of others. The goal is to have enough means of communicating that allow different people to choose the format that they like and are willing to give and receive information. The breadth of avenues and formats also allow the leader to give and receive different types of communication.

The fourth and final aspect of communication is monitoring and evaluation of the first three, that is, giving, receiving, and the system. Leaders must periodically evaluate the quantity and quality of the communication within the organization, as well as outside the organization.

Analysis Questions for Communication

- Did others get my intended meaning?
- Have I fully understood what others are trying to say?
- How many people are utilizing the various avenues for communication?
- Have I reached my entire intended audience?
- Is there a safe and open system for communication?
- How can I improve communication?

4. Conflict and Issue Resolution

Administrators are faced with the classic disagreement between individual needs and organizational expectations; consequently, they spend a substantial amount of time attempting to mediate conflict (Hoy & Miskel, 2001). In self-assessments conducted in graduate leadership classes, the authors of this text found that most students initially avoided conflict. To the novice, this makes perfect sense—who wants to be in a conflict? The wise leader, however, views every conflict as an opportunity—an opportunity to improve the organizational effectiveness, improve the quality of life for some or all of the organization's members, and an opportunity to better know and understand each other.

Conflict is inevitable and should warn the leader that a problem exists. Although unique situations may warrant different practices, the ideal approach is to problem-solve collaboratively. Kenneth Thomas (1976) identified five styles of managing conflict: *competing, collaborating, compromising, avoiding,* and *accommodating*. Competing is similar to a directive style, where a directive must be given, regardless of the competing belief. Compromising works well in the short-term, but it usually does not totally resolve the conflict. Accommodating is necessary when the leader is wrong or simply willing to give in to the other side. Avoiding is seldom recommended, except for buying time for things to "cool off" or gather additional information. The collaborating style uses problem-solving strategies and is the most often recommended style.

The two major areas of conflict facing leaders are conflict over differing expectations of roles and differing beliefs that, if not resolved, become issues. Role conflict can take the form of the classic model developed by Getzels (1958), where the personal needs of individuals conflict with the needs/expectations of the organization. These conflicts arise in numerous and varied ways. For example, the school may expect a teacher to work with others in a group or team-teach, whereas the teacher prefers to work alone. Conflict usually occurs when individuals believe that another is acting outside of his/her role or not fulfilling the expectations of the role. One might hear, "He is not supposed to do that" or "She is not doing her job." It is imperative that the leader and followers have a mutual understanding of the expectations of the various roles within the school/district. Both job descriptions and performance evaluations must be aligned and conform to the agreed-upon expectations of the particular role.

Issue resolution is another skill essential to leadership. Issues develop out of differing opinions or beliefs on a host of topics, such as policy, practice, goals, the means for reaching goals, values, and so forth. The wise leader welcomes issues and views them as an opportunity for improvement and better understanding of all parties. As with role conflict, problem solving approaches work best. Typically, the leader seeks consensus on the goals of either side of an issue and ensures both sides fully understand the opposing position. The leader then solicits all concerns and attempts to find a different and better solution that either side proposes. In this manner, when one side is in favor of Plan A and their opposing side is either in favor of Plan B or simply against Plan A, the leader seeks a Plan C.

Plan C is a different and better plan, because it has a unity of goals and has addressed all voiced concerns. In theory, if both sides have agreed on the goals and all concerns have been addressed, then the leader should have support from everyone. The main problems inherent in issue resolution are training staff to positively interact and "learn" from each other and be open to change (a better plan), and having a leader skilled in listening and guiding the parties to resolution.

It should be noted that this type of resolution relies on reasoning from all parties. There are some positions, however, that are taken without reasoning. In some cases, individuals are for or against because of deep-seated values. The sex education debate is an example of a conflict that involves the core beliefs and values of some of the parties. Reasoning often has little effect on instilled values. Another case is when one or more parties take a position on feelings, dreams, intuition, and the like. For example, you may find some people on either side of an issue that have a strong "gut" feelings that override their reasoning. Again, reasoning has minimal impact. In other instances, there is not enough information to support or predict the outcome of either side's proposed solution. For example, the conflicting research on the effectiveness of phonics versus whole language prevents any conclusion by reasoning alone. In cases like these where reasoning will not solve the problem, recognizing obstacles such as deep-seated values, intuitive feelings, and lack of evidence will help you develop a more appropriate strategy for a resolution.

Analysis Questions for Conflict and Issue Resolution

◆ Do all persons within the organization understand the duties and responsibilities of their position and the positions of others?

◆ Are expectations for others realistic and aligned with job descriptions?

◆ Is conflict seen as an opportunity?

◆ Have steps been taken to resolve personal conflict and/or issue conflict? Have steps moved both sides toward a different and better solution (rather than defensive argument of current positions)?

◆ What actions should be taken to address concerns from the above questions to solve the current problem and avoid similar problems in the future?

Future school leaders must utilize research, practice, reflect, and form habits of resolving conflict and issues.

5. Motivation

No human venture succeeds without strongly motivated men and women (Gardner, 1990). The wise leader understands that there is no universal motivation for every individual, but seeks to discover what motivates the people that he/she leads. There are many theories on motivation, and each may be partly true for some people. A brief overview of some of the major theories is presented here for the intern to consider for better understanding and use.

Before presenting theories for consideration and use, one should note what not to consider or use. There is a deep tradition of behavioral thinking in public schools. For all practical purposes, behavioral theories are not accepted or used by most psychologists. The field has moved past Pavlov and Skinner, who believed that the key to increasing motivation is to provide consistent and appropriate consequences to reinforce desired behaviors. Alfie Kohn challenged the reliance on rewards to motivate individuals with his provocative 1993 book, *Punished by Rewards*. He contends that hundreds of studies have shown that rewards produce only temporary compliance and that no lasting change in attitudes or behaviors can be attributed to the use of rewards. Cameron and Pierce (1997) used meta-analysis to asses the impact of reward as studied by all research performed since the 1970s, and they concluded that rewards are not inherently bad or good for people. Control over others and the manipulation of reality is inappropriate and unethical. Unfortunately, many school leaders wonder, "What rewards and punishments can we use to induce others to act appropriately?" Leaders need to move from behavioral perspectives to cognitive ones.

One of these cognitive theories is Attribution Theory, developed by Weiner (1986). Attribution Theory is simply based on exactly what an individual attributes to his/her success or failure. When something happens, an individual can make two explanations for it: an external attribution or an internal attribution. An external attribution assigns causality to an outside agent or force, and an internal attribution assigns causality to factors within the person. Attribution Theory contends that high achievers attribute their successes and failures to factors within themselves and their control. The key to improving motivation according to Attribution Theory is to help the person develop a self-attribution explanation of effort for their success or failure.

Cognitive Dissonance Theory, proposed by Festinger (1957), details ideas similar to the disequilibrium described by Piaget's theory of cognitive development. Festinger's theory states that when there is a discrepancy between two beliefs, two actions, or a belief and an action, people will act to resolve the conflict and discrepancies. To motivate people to act, one must create the appropriate amount of disequilibrium.

Expectancy Theory, attributed to Vroom (1964), proposes the following equation to determine motivation: Motivation = Perceived Probability (Expectancy) x Connection of Success and Reward (Instrumentality) x Value of Obtaining the Goal (Valance/Value). The equation details the idea that motivation is the product of a person's belief that he/she can be successful at the task, the degree of connection that he/she sees between the activity and success, and how much he/she values the results of success. All three of these variables must be high in order for an individual to be motivated.

Maslow (1954) developed the Hierarchy of Human Needs to detail his theory of human motivation. Maslow contends that individuals have a hierarchy of needs that motivate their behavior. People are motivated to attend to and satisfy their needs for physiological satisfaction, safety, belongingness and love, esteem, and self-actualization. Individuals are motivated to satisfy these needs in this order. The leader's responsibility is to provide for lower level needs and assist members of the organization to reach higher levels.

Alderfer (1972) developed a hierarchy of three human needs. These needs included the basic need for existence, the need for relatedness, and the need for growth. Alderfer, like Maslow, contends that individuals are inherently motivated to satisfy these needs, and that organizations and schools should work to ensure that many of their employees' and students' needs are met to ensure proper motivation.

William Glasser (1985) identified five basic needs: the need for belonging, power, fun, freedom, and survival. The need for belonging is described as the need for involvement with people, to love and be loved, and to affiliate and bond with other people. The need for power is described as the need for achievement and accomplishment—a sense of being in control of his or her own life. The need for fun is the need to enjoy life, laugh, and see humor. The need for freedom is the need to make choices and live without undue restraint. The need for survival is the need to maintain life and good health, including the basic needs of comfort, food, shelter, water, and the like.

Fredrick Herzberg (1959) proposed the Motivation and Hygiene Theory, which divides elements that determine an organization's ability to motivate its employees into two sections, hygiene and motivational issues. Herzberg contends that hygiene issues can't motivate employees, but they can minimize dissatisfaction. Hygiene issues include policies, supervision, salary, interpersonal relations, and working conditions. Motivators create satisfaction by fulfilling an individual's needs for meaning and personal growth. Herzberg identified achievement, recognition, the work itself, responsibility, and advancement as individual motivators. The best way to help motivate an individual is to ensure that both hygiene and motivational issues and needs are met.

Bandura's (1986) Social Cognition Theory proposes reciprocal determination as a primary factor in both learning and motivation. Bandura contends that the environment (an individual's behavior) and the individual's characteristics (an individual's knowledge, emotions, and cognitive development) both influence and are influenced by each other. Two components of Bandura's Social Cognition Theory affect an individual's learning and motivation: self-efficacy and self-regulation. Self-efficacy involves a person's belief that a particular action is possible and that the he or she can successfully accomplish the action. Self-regulation involves the person's ability to establish goals, to develop a plan to attain the goals, to display the commitment needed to implement the plan, and to reflect on and modify the plan if needed. To increase motivation, one must provide for and support another's self-efficacy and self-regulatory needs. The more individuals believe they will be successful, and the better able they are to regulate their goals and plans, the more motivated they will be.

McClelland's (1961) Achievement Motivation Theory asserts three basic motivational human needs: achievement, power, and affiliation. McClelland's need for achievement includes an individual's need for feedback, the need to take moderate risks, the need for personal responsibility, and the need for success. The need for power is rooted in an individual's need for influence over his own life and others. An individual's need for affiliation is based on the human needs for acceptance, friendship, love, and his or her desire to cooperate with others. The leader's responsibility is to provide for all three but focus on achievement.

Ames (1992) and Maehr and Midgley (1991) also focused on achievement motivation with their Goal Theory. The Goal Theory of Motivation states that one's success is determined by the reasons or purposes an individual perceives for achieving. The theory identifies two types of goals: task goals and ability goals. When pursuing task goals, the motivation is personal improvement or understanding, and the focus is on mastering skills and knowledge. When pursuing ability goals, the motivation is to demonstrate one's ability, and the focus is on appearing competent. Goal theorists have made recommendations that schools work toward task goals and away from ability goals in classrooms. They propose that schools move away from recognition for relative performance, honor rolls for high grades, and overuse of praise. They should move toward recognition of progress improvement with emphasis on learning for its own sake to motivate students.

The intern must be knowledgeable of motivation theory and attempt to increase motivation. Rewards and coercive behavior modification may show temporary results but also may cause harm. The key is to understand what motivates each member of the organization.

Analysis Questions for Motivation

♦ Are the needs of the people being met?

♦ Are the needs of the people in line with the needs or the organization?

♦ What processes are used to motivate? Are they effective?

♦ What actions need to be taken to address any concerns from the above questions to solve the current problem and avoid similar problems in the future?

Future school leaders must utilize research, practice, reflect, and form habits of providing for motivation for everyone they lead.

6. Group Processes

Warren Bennis (2000) believes that our world is the product of "Great Groups," teams of creative persons who banded together to achieve remarkable successes that would not have been possible through a traditional hierarchical approach. The research on group processes in schools finds that leaders who trust and believe in others and model these traits will accomplish far more and develop devoted followers (Hoyle, English & Steffy, 1990). But, if success in leadership is defined as "the ability to get groups of people to work toward the accomplishment of the vision, mission, and goals for the district/school," most educational leaders do not meet that definition. Traditionally, schools are organizations where work is done individually.

Breaking with this tradition and reforming the culture where faculty and administrators collaboratively work toward school improvement requires commitment to empowerment, developing new leaders, cooperation, and shared responsibility. Leaders must invest time, effort, and expertise to overcome traditions, past failures, and lack of interest and/or expertise on the part of faculty (and administrators) to work together.

Teachers in graduate educational leadership programs often admit to very negative perspectives and past experiences in the use of teams, committees, and groups. "All they wanted us to do was to come up with what they wanted in the first place." "We worked very hard and then they did not accept our recommendation." "They refuse to listen to any problem or complaint." "Why should we do their job?" "We have enough to do without doing extra work." Overcoming these negative attitudes is a difficult, but not impossible task.

The intern should remember that to change an attitude, one must change a belief. To change a belief, one must experience something new. Thus, it is the responsibility of the leader to provide new positive experiences in working in groups with shared goals, shared responsibility, shared authority, and shared decision making. Many studies on group work describe how leaders should conduct meetings and train staff to work in groups.

Meetings should be called only when there is a need to meet. Calling in the entire faculty to announce what could have been put in writing is insulting and a waste of time. In this instance, there is no need to meet. Likewise, calling a meeting to discuss failures of a few faculty wastes the time of all others. The need to meet should be common sense. Meeting involves discussion, learning, group thinking, and group work. Obviously, a leader should develop a set of principles or rules for meetings and use effective skills in conducting the meeting.

The following is an example of rules for meetings:

♦ Schedule meetings only when necessary and there is a need to meet. It is advised, however, that the leader not go for long periods of time without meeting with staff. Information that can be put in writing should be communicated through e-mail, memos, or other means of two-way communication between meetings.

♦ Prior to the meeting, distribute an agenda with purpose, time, and location listed. Participants in meetings should come prepared, having read or considered items to be discussed in the meeting. Also, the leader should give staff the opportunity to request items for the agenda. The leader should allow time to decide or discuss additions to the agenda. It is important that all faculty members know that they have a say in their meetings and that their input is valued.

♦ Meetings should be arranged and organized for participation. The leader may use a circle or semicircle seating plan or at least stand or sit on the same level.

♦ The leader should solicit participation from and show interest in individual members. He/she should model listening skills and value the comments and conflicting perspectives from the members.

♦ The leader should stay on time and on task. Often, leaders plan for more than can be accomplished at one meeting. Thus, time management is vital, and the leader is responsible for keeping to the item or task at hand. It is also the responsibility of the leader to begin and end on time. Most staff developers recommend ending meetings a few minutes early. People tend to quit listening if meetings go beyond the scheduled ending time. It is also poor modeling for the leader to keep meetings past the announced time.

♦ The leader summarizes accomplishments of the meeting and follows up on decisions. Followers quickly lose respect and trust in leaders that speak well but do not follow up. Followers expect meetings to produce results. Follow-up is crucial in establishing a culture where meetings are viewed as important and productive.

Faculty members meet at other times than in leader-called meetings. These may be grade-level or subject-area department meetings, committees, task forces, or a host of other types of groups. If the leader expects these meetings to be productive, training must be given. Members need guidelines, adequate information, and clear understanding of purposes and goals; and they must learn to work in a group situation. These groups may have an assigned leader, such as the department chair, or the task may be assigned and a leader may emerge. Often different faculty members have different expertise and skills, and a different person may become the leader according to the topics or tasks.

Regardless of the type of group meeting or whether a leader is assigned, members of the group will need to formalize their own set of rules. How much time will be used? Do we need goal consensus and/or consensus on the final recommendation? Are we meeting to learn more about the topic and each other, or are we here to argue and defend our opinions? Is interrupting and judging other's comments allowed? Do we agree to have equal responsibility? Productive groups do not just happen. They must be developed.

As previously written, great things can be accomplished by getting groups of people to work together. The time and effort given by the leader in developing this type of culture pays great dividends in the long term. To overcome many negative attitudes of meetings, committees, and working groups, the leader must truly believe in others and their abilities to accomplish tasks and make effective decisions. Never pretend to give groups responsibility or authority. Always be completely honest.

Analysis Questions for Group Processes

- ◆ Have the formal and informal groups been identified?
- ◆ Are all groups working productively and collaboratively?
- ◆ Are goals for the groups realistic, understood, and acceptable?
- ◆ Is trust and freedom of expression the norm of all groups?
- ◆ Are meetings used effectively and efficiently?
- ◆ What actions need to be taken to address any concerns from the above questions to solve the current problem and avoid similar problems in the future?

It is imperative that future school leaders utilize research, practice, reflect, and form habits of effective group processes to solicit support, develop new leaders, and reach organizational goals.

7. Leadership Style and Power

For decades, researchers have studied leadership style and power. They have coined many terms to describe leadership style. Dunn and Dunn (1977) listed seven styles: collaborative, cooperative, participative, bureaucratic, laissez-faire, benevolent despot, and autocratic. Most recently, Goleman (2000) devised six terms that described various styles used by business leaders: coercive, authoritative/commanding, affiliative, democratic, pacesetting, and coaching. He called coercive and pacesetting negative and the other four positive.

In combination of these and others, we will use six styles to consider for appropriate use:

1. *Directive*. Similar to authoritative, autocratic, or commanding, this style is used when strict compliance is needed or it is an urgent/emergency situation. The directive style is appropriate for quick changes or guidance. It is also appropriate when only the leader has the necessary knowledge or expertise.

2. *Participative*. Often labeled democratic, this style is used when limited time is available and/or the leader holds most of the account-

ability for the results. With this style, the leader makes the final decision or approves policy or practice but gathers input from others. Ideally, this involves all those affected by the decision or action.

3. *Collaborative*. Also labeled democratic, this is the ideal style and is a means of working in true collaboration with others. This style values others' expertise and helps develop future leaders. This style requires adequate time, training, and a shared responsibility. In most cases, better decisions are made with the use of a collaborative style.

4. *Coaching*. The leader remains in a leader/teacher/mentor role with the subordinate. This is also an ideal style when followers are not prepared for true collaboration. Coaching frees the subordinate to practice as a leader, while remaining under the guidance and assistance of the formal leader.

5. *Affiliative*. This style is appropriate when the leader has more concern for the person or persons than the task. This could be when trying to build positive relationships or persons are dealing with personal issues. Once the personal problem has passed or the relationship has been formed, the leader can focus on the task and use a coaching or collaborative style. It should be noted that this is opposite of Goleman's pacesetting style, where the task takes precedence over people.

6. *Laissez-Faire*. This style is seldom recommended, but may be appropriate for minor tasks where followers have more expertise and interest than the leader.

The key to using the most effective style is to know the situation and people and strive to meet the needs of both. In some cases, the entire staff must be dealt with using a very directive style and at other times, only some of the staff needs a directive style. In some cases, some of the staff needs coaching, while others are at a level of collaboration. The main lesson is that people and situations, not the leader's preferences, dictate what style the leader should use.

A leader must also wield power to accomplish great things. Although many believe power corrupts or no person should have power over another, power can be both positive and negative. The wise leader understands the negative potential of power but strives to use power for good. In the classic model of power, French and Raven (1959) believe there are five basic types of power: reward, coercive, legitimate, referent, and expert.

1. The use of *reward power* is tempting. Many believe it is right to reward others for their effort and feel a sense of joy in giving to those that deserve it. However, the use of reward power can do more harm than good. In giving rewards to some, others are overlooked.

In giving rewards, some begin to expect it and may only work for reward or limit their efforts to the criteria set for the reward. Additionally, it is impossible to find a reward that everyone is willing to work for. The reward system becomes a game, and many tire of playing. The end result is that the leader's power is diminished. Use of reward power is not recommended.

2. *Coercive power* is an obvious misuse of power. Yet, coercive power is integral to dealing with students. Making threats to children for misbehavior or poor academic performance carries over to administration, and threats are then made to faculty and staff. The use of coercive power is unethical. Coercion and punishment do not solve problems in schools. The wise leader refrains from using either reward or coercive power.

3. *Legitimate power* is derived from the authority given to the position. Superintendents have authority over principals; principals, authority over teachers; and teachers, authority over students. Depending on the history and culture of the district, however, the power given to a position may vary. Some teachers have very little power over students, and some principals exert minimal power over the faculty. It is others that give power to the leader, so is he/she cannot depend solely on the power of the position.

The wise leader understands both the powers inherent to the position and the powers *not* given to the position. As previously mentioned in the section on role conflict, it is vital for the leader to act within the laws, policies, and traditions for his/her position. Abuse of power causes conflict, and refusal to use power is a failure to fulfill the responsibilities of the position. The leader is responsible for knowing and acting within the appropriate range of their legitimate power or authority.

So far, we have recommended against the use of two types of power and recommended the limited use of another. If leaders want additional power to accomplish great things, they must seek to expand their referent and/or expert power.

4. *Referent power* is the ideal. Followers give power to leaders that they identify with, believe in, and trust. To increase referent power, the leader must know others and allow them to know him or her. The leader must work with others, find consensus in the vision, and determine the means of achieving the vision. Gaining referent power requires effective communication and a strong belief in the value of others and working together.

5. Possessing special knowledge or skill creates *expert power*. Followers freely give power to experts for help and guidance. To increase expert power, the leader must commit time and effort to become more expert in essential areas of leadership and education. These may include expertise in curriculum, technology, instruction, school operations, communication, and a host of other possibilities. The wise leader seeks additional expertise in all areas but focuses on the greatest strengths and needs of others.

It should be noted that the omission of political power is purposeful. Political power is group power derived from the exchange of favors for personal gain. Although every organization has some degree of political activity, the wise leader does not seek personal gain but gain for others and the organization. Political leadership is an oxymoron. The intern must be aware of politics, so as not to be abused by it, but must avoid seeking political power or taking any leadership position solely for personal gain.

The final aspect of power is empowerment. Most of the research today recommends teacher empowerment (Rice & Schneider, 1994; Marks & Louis, 1997; Rinehart, Short, & Johnson, 1997; Rinehart, Short, Short, & Eckley, 1998). The wise leader understands that empowering others in the quest for school improvement builds a broad power base. If one gives out power, he/she gains power. Only in politics would one view this as giving up power. Empowering others builds support, buy-in, consensus, and the development of current and future leaders.

Analysis Questions for Leadership Style and Power

♦ Has the appropriate style been used in this particular situation and with differing people?

- *Directive* (authoritarian, commanding): legal mandate; very little time, interest and/or expertise of the followers; low need for quality and/or support for decision; higher need for task than people

- *Participative* (democratic): limited time, limited expertise of leader, limited interest and/or expertise of followers, some degree of quality and support needed

- *Collaborative* (democratic, shared decision making): adequate time available, high degree of interest and expertise of followers, high need for quality and support, desire for developing followers

- *Coaching*: adequate time; need to increase interest and expertise of followers, desire to develop followers and future leaders, need for support and assistance to individuals, higher need for people than task.
- *Affiliative*: total concern for needs of people versus task
- *Laissez-Faire* (complete delegation): adequate time, high degree of interest and expertise of followers, low level of interest and/or expertise of leader, low need for quality of decision, desire to let others lead

♦ Has the appropriate power been used?

- Reward—recommended only for achieving goals, never for political gain
- Coercive—recommended only in emergency situations
- Expert—used when leader has high degree of expertise over followers
- Legitimate (Position, Legal Authority)—used to fulfill requirements of position
- Referent—used for consensus building and support

♦ What actions need to be taken to address any concerns from above to solve the current problem and avoid similar problems in the future?

It is imperative that future school leaders utilize research, practice, reflect, and form habits of using appropriate style and power to reach organizational goals and positively and ethically meet the needs of everyone they lead.

8. Culture and Climate

The only thing of real importance that leaders do is to create and mange culture (Schein, 1992). This is best understood when one considers that the school's vision, ways of making decisions and communicating, amount and type of conflict, degree of motivation, use of power, and the ability to change are all ingredients of the culture. People form attitudes (Greenberg and Baron, 1997) or an ideology (Mintzberg, 1989) about the values, norms, expectations, and practices that set their school apart from others. The culture also includes the history, traditions, and beliefs of the organization, and the relative importance of each.

The leader is responsible for understanding the culture. He/she realizes that culture changes over time and that subcultures exist. The wise leader assesses the past and current culture and seeks consensus for improvement. Cultural changes take time, need a shared commitment, and require extensive follow-up for the change to become an accepted aspect of the new culture.

The leader can use formal assessments from business or principal organizations, for example, National Association for Secondary School Principals and/or National Association of Elementary School Principals. Or, they can assess current needs or issues. How does the organization promote diversity, support staff development, recognize progress, and invite parent involvement? What beliefs underlie these issues? Are the policies and practices aligned with the mission? What can be learned from other schools in our country and abroad? Once the culture is understood, steps can be taken to improve it.

Studies indicate that the most effective schools are distinguished by outstanding social climate—not by elaborate facilities, extensively trained teachers, small classes, or high levels of financial support (Erickson, 1981). School climate is simply defined as the feelings or atmosphere of the school. Climate can change quickly and often. The leader must always be aware of the climate and take action if the current climate is negative.

The leader should be proactive in dealing with climate. The leader can use formal assessments, develop trusting relationships, have effective means for communicating, and seek to know the feelings and atmosphere on a daily basis. The leader should be very sensitive to and take responsibility for staff and student morale. He or she should investigate the causes for low morale and the steps that can be taken to raise morale.

Climate and culture are extremely important aspects for measuring the *quality of life* in the school. Quality of life affects academic performance, behavior, staff turnover, motivation, health, and the mental health of all members of the school. The wise leader sets culture and climate as a high priority.

Analysis Questions for Culture and Climate

- ♦ Are there conflicts/concerns with the current organizational culture?

- ♦ If so, have adequate time and resources been allocated in developing a new culture?

- ♦ Are there concerns with the current climate?

- ♦ Have adequate assessments been conducted to accurately assess the climate?

- ♦ What actions need to be taken to address any concerns from the above questions to solve the current problem and avoid similar problems in the future?

Future school leaders must utilize research, practice, reflect, and form habits of assessing, improving, and creating a positive school culture and climate.

9. Change

Successful leaders initiate and manage change. Of all of the skills presented in this text, leading change is the most difficult. Michael Fullan (2001) asserts that there are two main aspects of educational change: what changes to implement (theories of education) and how to implement change (theories of change). They interact and shape each other, but the critical factor is the distinctiveness of the individual setting. What works in one setting may not work in another.

+ What do we know about change?
+ It is a process that takes place over time (2–3 years).
+ The process has steps or stages.
+ It must begin with the individual, then spread out to the organization.
+ It requires a change in belief.
+ It is difficult and seldom worth the effort.
+ Most changes fail.
+ A real need or pressure is required.
+ Not everyone will change.
+ No amount of information will make the change totally clear.
+ It will always have disagreement and conflict.
+ Improvement cannot occur without it.
+ The leader has a key role in facilitating.
+ Those affected by change must be involved in the process
+ It must be evaluated and monitored from beginning to end.

The most startling aspect cited in the list above is that most change efforts fail. Most experts recommend attempting only one or two changes at a time. The wise leader must fully understand the change process and choose his/her change efforts wisely. Most people fear and/or resist change. Change causes disequilibrium in individuals and they seek the balance of the past.

What are the factors in resistance to change?

+ Some agree with new programs but never do anything.
+ Some agree change is needed but only in another department.

- Some want to be last—they hope it dies out before reaches them.
- Some need more time—they rationalize resistance.
- Some are against any change made from a state or national level or any change that is not local.
- Some only rely on costs—is it worth the time and effort.
- Some want incremental change—anything new that is just like the old.
- Some are fearful of change and their security.
- Some are successful and are very conservative toward change.
- Some lack the skill to make the change.
- Some have an honest difference of opinion.

Leaders can take appropriate actions to reduce resistance in spite of these factors. These include:

- Allow teachers to feel the change is their own.
- Show that the change reduces rather than increases their burdens.
- Reach consensus on the value of the change.
- Involve those that have an interest in the change.
- Validate and recognize objections.
- Give feedback and clarification.
- Develop support, trust, and confidence with those involved.
- Be open to revision and improvement.
- Set attainable and realistic goals.
- Change and resistance to change are inevitable: The leader must guide and direct it.

Successful change efforts

- Have broad-based ownership, including informal and formal power
- Have positive relationships already built
- Have support from administration
- Have community awareness
- Fit philosophy, mission, and culture of school
- Have a moral purpose
- Are relevant to those affected

- Have a planning and evaluation stage
- Have adequate resources available
- Are monitored and adjusted in process
- Include more training during implementation than at beginning
- Have few, if any, other big changes occurring at the same time

These lists were complied from the works of Robert Evans (1996); Gay Hendricks and Kate Ludeman (1996); Peter Senge et al. (1996); Tony Wagner (1994); Hall and Hord (2001); and Michael Fullan (2002). It should be noted that the lack of any one variable might cause the change to fail.

It has been said that change is the only constant in life. It has also been said that everyone wants improvement, but no one wants change. The skill of effecting change is one that requires much thought, analysis, and effort. Despite the hurdles, if one is to lead, one must lead change.

Analysis Questions for Change

- Is the change proposed only one of a few?
- Is there a moral purpose in the new change?
- Do all involved understand the change process?
- Have positive relationships been built?
- Is the creation and sharing of information a priority?
- Has a productive disturbance and a subsequent coherence been accomplished?
- Have steps been taken to reduce resistance?
- Have the factors that produce success been implemented?
- What actions need to be taken to address any concerns from the above questions to solve the current problem and avoid similar problems in the future?

Future school leaders must utilize research, practice, reflect, and form habits of leading educational change.

10. Evaluation

The topic of evaluation is complex and controversial, and it involves many entities, subjects, criteria, and beliefs. The federal government, unions, accrediting agencies, boards of education, universities, real estate agencies, the press, and a host of professional organizations all rate and evaluate public schools.

One might conclude that so many others get involved because we educators do a poor job of it.

If anything is worth doing, it is worth evaluating and finding improvements. Only through meaningful evaluation can strengths, weaknesses, conflicting efforts, and wasteful efforts emerge and allow leaders to analyze and take appropriate actions. Ratings and labeling do little to find answers. Evaluation must be thorough, having adequate breadth and depth.

Evaluations should be administered on the following:

- Personnel
- Students
- Programs
- Curriculum and instruction
- Testing
- Technology
- School/district goals and plans
- Community and parent relations
- Student and staff retention
- Staff development
- Food service
- Transportation
- Extra- and cocurricular activities
- Facilities and safety
- Fiscal accountability
- Legal compliance
- Decision making
- Communication
- Conflict and issue resolution
- Motivation
- Groups working collaboratively
- Leadership style and power
- Culture and climate
- Change efforts

♦ Evaluation processes and measures

This list is not exhaustive, but it does show the scope of what needs evaluation. Only through evaluative information can leaders plan appropriate action for improvement. The evaluation must begin with the existing practice and measure the extent of progress toward the vision or final goal. Beginning, formative, and summative measures should be taken at appropriate intervals. Care must be taken to choose evaluative instruments that reliably measure what you intend to measure.

The new trend in educational leadership is toward data-driven decisions. Many new books are published to assist leaders in improving skills in collecting, analyzing, and using data for plans and decisions. It is highly recommended that future leaders study and develop new skills in the use of evaluative data.

Analysis Questions for Evaluation

♦ Are effective personnel and program evaluations established?

♦ Are both formative and summative evaluations utilized?

♦ Is data from evaluations used for decisions and planning?

♦ What actions need to be taken to address any concerns from the above questions to solve the current problem and avoid similar problems in the future?

It is imperative that future school leaders utilize research, practice, reflect, and form habits of effective evaluation.

The intent of this book is that interns should begin their internship or training with an in-depth evaluation of their knowledge, skill, and past performance. They are further expected to monitor and utilize on going evaluation of their progress and conclude with a thorough summative evaluation. The next sections will assist interns with ongoing reflection and evaluation. Stage Four provides the criteria for the summative evaluation.

3.3   Reflection in Action

Reflection as a Route to Expertise

Experts do not face isolated problems but changing situations involving complexly interwoven themes. Expertise develops as the result of *reflective skills*, the ability to think more deeply about a problem, and the ability to take action or make adjustments accordingly. Experts are people with content-specific knowledge (Shulman, 1986; Bransford et al, 2000). The expert not only masters a knowledge base but also understands the circumstances in which it is applied. This expertise cannot be gained by being told what to do; it is more than mastering a handful of general principles. Expertise is part of a complex performance rather than a discrete piece of information. Experts take action and make adjustments as they go. They also reconsider their actions after the fact.

Administrative actions cannot be reduced to a fixed set of principles about "what works" or a handful of generalized rules. Administrative practice is a complex art that combines thinking abstractly, weighing of prior experience, and taking action. It is more like driving a taxi cab in New York City, in which the performance involves keeping the final destination in mind, while making multiple adjustments based on weather, time of day, traffic, accidents, advice of passengers, and so forth. No two performances are ever exactly the same because no two sets of conditions are ever exactly alike. Expertise comes from the combination of action and reflection. Expertise is gained as one learns to adjust the performance based on the factors and one's experiences with them. Learning from one's prior actions (and mistakes) is basic to the development of expertise.

Novices often feel clumsy and unsure of themselves; they need help in thinking about problems of practice and how to use prior knowledge to determine what actions to take. One strategy focuses on the cognitive strategies used by experts. In the school administration area, this focus helps make the thinking and problem-solving skills of school leaders more explicit and available to scrutiny (Hallinger, Leithwood, & Murphy, 1993; Leithwood & Steinbach 1993; 1995).

What Expert Leaders Do Better Than Novices

Leaders acquire many skills as they progress from novice to expert. Leaders learn to

- ◆ Recognize the perspectives of others
- ◆ Accommodate how others learn
- ◆ Understand how hierarchy filters information
- ◆ Anticipate problems
- ◆ Prioritize relevant detail
- ◆ Be comfortable with ambiguity

For most people, these processes are performed internally. Self-evaluation leads to scrutiny, discussion, and analysis of these expert processes. Reflection allows people to learn from their experiences, and administrative skills are acquired through a combination of theory and practice.

What are some of the defining characteristics of these expert performances? One area of study concerns how leaders deal with ambiguous conditions. Wagner (1993) suggests that many problems faced by leaders

♦ Are ill defined

♦ Are formulated by oneself

♦ Require additional information

♦ Have no single correct solution

♦ Involve multiple methods for obtaining multiple solutions

♦ Involve everyday experience

Experts apply tacit knowledge, a kind of practical know-how that guides how problems are managed on a day-to-day basis.

Cognitive Processes of Leadership

How do leaders learn to make decisions? Yekovich (1993) suggests that cognitive skills required in making decisions occur in distinct stages. The first stage is the *declarative stage*, in which the individual learns concepts and facts, which are then stored in memory as declarative knowledge. The declarative knowledge base is a loosely connected set of information; as more domain-related information is acquired, there is an increase in expertise.

The second stage is the *associative stage*, which is characterized by two noticeable changes in the knowledge state of the individual: (1) There is growth in declarative knowledge, and (2) more importantly, the organization and interconnectedness of knowledge becomes more expert. The continual development of the knowledge base allows leaders (experts) to associate facts and concepts with actions and operations in an arena of practice. This is the beginning of the movement from declarative knowledge (knowledge about) to procedural knowledge (how-to knowledge).

The final stage, the *autonomous stage*, is more of a fine-tuning stage in which there are elaboration and interconnectedness in the network. Fine-tuning also refers to the generalization and discrimination to allow for an appropriate degree of generality or specificity; the algorithms used to make decisions become more automatic (hence the term *autonomous*). This often occurs without awareness, and uses few cognitive resources of the decision maker. (Yekovich, 1993, 151–153).

Decision making is also connected to the ability to make midcourse adjustments. Expertise relates to the leader's skill or ability to adjust and modify the explanatory models being used as new and discrepant experiences are faced. Glidewell (1993) discusses several factors concerning how leaders make these adjustments (or how and when CEOs change their minds). He looks at *celerity factors* (the *speed* of the midcourse changes), *background factors* (the size, nature, and competitiveness of the organization), and *personal factors* (age, previously held beliefs, pragmatism, mood of the leader, resources at issue). Successful organizational leaders in the study were able to compartmentalize their prior experience in ways that allowed them to change their conceptual frameworks and mental models of what was going on and what needed to be done.

Limits to Experience

Allison and Allison (1993) report that direct experience in the role of school administrator, even for a short time, enables novices to increase attention to the details of presented problems. However, veteran administrators in their study did worse, compared to practitioners with less experience, on some of the problems presented. This suggests that experience alone does not guarantee best practice. Novices would do well to consider both the advantages and limits of experience.

Conclusion

King and Ketchener (1994) believe reflective thinking is characterized by a view that knowledge is not a given but instead must be actively constructed within a specific context, and that individuals reasoning at these stages understand that conclusions must be grounded in relevant data and remain open to reevaluation. They argue that this kind of thinking is what Dewey (1938) called reflective thinking or reflective judgment.

Reflection is learning to analyze prior experiences to better understand how they shape future courses of action; it is thinking about how actions are connected to cultural norms, to initial experiences growing up, institutional histories, and on-the-job experience. Reflection provides a way to access the more complete story that people bring with them to their performances. It builds expertise by tapping experience and simultaneously recognizing the limits of its application.

The intern must begin to develop the art of reflection in practice and reflection on practice. This includes reflecting on decisions and actions, making changes and adjustments, and making mistakes. You should practice asking yourself the following:

- What facts/concepts, that is, mental models are you using?

- What prior beliefs are you assuming to be truth?

- What history and/or traditions of the district/school are pressuring belief and action?

- What are the effects of your emotional state or mood?

- How does the availability or lack of resources affect your actions?

- How have on-the-job experiences affected belief and action?

Reflective thinking must be practiced and nurtured if you would like to move from novice leader to expert leader. It is highly recommended that the intern make daily or weekly notes on their use and progress in reflective practice.

3.4 Enrichment Activities

Developing and improving leadership skills by using vignettes can provide a safe harbor for both the emerging and practicing leader to explore the application of theory, knowledge, skills, and dispositions to resolve a wide variety of difficult leadership dilemmas. Reading, researching, seeking expert opinion, and reflecting on the issues imbedded in vignettes provide an excellent approach to learning and developing a strong leadership advantage.

The following vignettes may be used as an enrichment activity. You may incorporate them into your internship plan or use them as learning activities for discussions with other interns as part of a course or a program. You should consult with your district or university program supervisor to decide whether to use this activity. In any case, it is highly recommended that interns attempt as many of these exercises as possible.

Read the vignettes, and write a brief response for each statement. Indicate why you agree or disagree with each vignette. After you complete your initial response to the statement, research the issues contained in the vignette and discuss the issues with an experienced administrator. Revise your response to include learning, insights, and comments you deem to be most useful. File your responses in your notebook for future reflection and reference.

Success for All Students: An Administrator's Responsibility

"Broken promises and forgotten children" perhaps best describes the plight of an ever-increasing number of children in schools today. Students born into unhealthy environments and raised on the painful edge of poverty and/or within the walls of troubled homes have little or no hope for a better future unless schools take the steps required to fill the void in their lives. Make no mistake about it: The No Child Left Behind Act (NCLB) is designed to hold schools, teachers, and school administrators accountable for the academic success of all children. Successful administrators believe that both children and society are best served by making this outcome a reality.

Questions for Reflection

What are the most serious obstacles to assuring academic success for at risk children in my school? Has my school identified the children who might be at risk academically? What specific steps has my school taken to support teachers and administrators in their effort to assure that all students (including at-risk children) succeed academically? What insights, concerns, or questions do you have regarding this statement?

Were the Schools of Yesterday Better?

Administrators and teachers hear complaints with increasing frequency regarding how poorly schools of today perform as compared to the schools of old, statements such as: "In my day our schools had superior academic standards," and "Students were better behaved and student achievement was far higher than is the case with the schools of today." Further, a growing number of citizens openly claim that the schools of yesterday produced far better results at a fraction of the cost than do the schools of today. To support this position, school critics point to a growing number of national reports that indicate that literacy rates are rapidly declining, drug abuse is on the increase, dropout rates are increasing at an alarming rate, and educators and schools are out of touch with the needs of society.

Questions for Reflection

Is there a fundamental difference between the schools of yesterday and today? Do the administrators and teachers in my school carefully identify the specific strengths in our academic programs and school services to build on them in ways that will facilitate higher levels of academic and social success for all of our students? What steps do I need to take to prepare myself to adequately respond to critics attacking the quality of our schools? What ideas, concerns, or questions do you have regarding this statement?

Cultural Bias and Standardized Tests

Standardized tests have nothing to do with culture, economic status, or race. The claim of a cultural bias in regard to standardized testing is off-base. These tests measure what a student has learned and nothing more. The truth is: Low-test scores reflect low levels of student learning. Knowledgeable educators understand that effective teaching and learning starts with diagnosing what students know or do not know. And standardized tests provide educators with a useful instrument to do just that. To claim that standardized tests don't measure student learning is nonsense. Schools teach children important information that can be used develop skills and knowledge. Standardized tests measure a child's level of achievement in the cognitive domain, and schools are best equipped to impart cognitive knowledge. Those who are concerned that using standardized tests will eventually lead to opening the door for test makers and the federal government to control the curriculum should know this: Washington and or test makers will be able to control the curriculum in the local school only to the extent we permit them to do so.

Questions for Reflection

To what extent is standardized testing used in my school? Do the teachers and administrators in my school understand the benefits and limits of using test results to inform teaching and learning decisions in my school? Are standard tests fair to students, or are they culturally biased? Will a mandate to use standardized tests to measure the academic achievement of students lead to the government and or the major test-publishing firms taking control of the local schools? What ideas, concerns, or questions do you have regarding this statement?

Evaluation Drives Successful Schooling, Not Money

Educational leaders want to provide the very best educational program possible for the children attending their schools. Unfortunately, some school leaders equate school funding with excellence. Nothing could be more mistaken. Improving the quality of education is not always a matter of wealth. Excellence can be made possible by evaluation and better allocation of existing school funding levels.

Questions for Reflection

What insights, concerns, or questions do you have regarding this statement? To what extent is the evaluation of programs, administrators, faculty, and staff used to improve the quality of education in my school? What ideas, concerns, or questions do you have regarding this statement?

Building Public Support

Power used in unethical ways always does damage to the climate for teaching and learning in the schools. The administrator should periodically evaluate his/her use of power to assure that the power associated with his/her position is not misused. This involves asking some hard questions. The administrator should determine whether he/she has taken any action to influence the outcome of a decision to benefit a close friend, family member, or a politically connected party (elected official, local business leader, special interest group, etc.). In addition to these questions, the administrator should ask if he/she has attempted to change the outcome of a disciplinary decision or assignment of a grade, or influence the awarding of contracts or the purchase school supplies. These are just a few examples of the manner in which administrator power is most often misused. Unethical use of power results in loss of community support, public trust, and in some cases, criminal charges being brought against the administrator. But perhaps even worse, the misuse of power always has a negative impact on children and the quality of education they are provided. In contrast, using administrative power in ethical ways results in building trust and support for schools and educators, and most important, it forms the foundation on which a strong climate for teaching and learning can be constructed.

Questions for Reflection

How would I react if I witnessed an administrator using power in unethical ways? What steps should an administrator take to assure that power is applied only in ethical ways? What role should board policy play in protecting against the misuse of power in the school? What insights, concerns, or questions do you have regarding this statement?

Responding to Charges of Molestation

Historically, the problem of improper student/staff relations, including molestation, was handled in a variety of ways. Some administrators simply ignored or dismissed any complaints. Others allowed the offending party to move on to another school, often with a good recommendation regarding his/her teaching ability. These administrators used such methods to deal child molestation to avoid embarrassment, which always accompanies charges of child molestation. To be sure, some administrators moved to terminate school employees—but termination was rare. "It's best to not air dirty laundry in public" approach was often used because it meant not having to deal with the problem. Some administrators attempt to justify this approach because of a mistaken belief that molestation charges are hard to prove without a complete investigation. They also mistakenly believe that an investigation and any subsequent litigation that results will be more hostile toward children than the adult involved, the adult will be believed rather than the child, the child's parents will not want their child exposed to further harm brought by way of an investigation and or legal action, or worse, they don't want to damage the career of an educator. Today, there are very serious consequences for those who fail to follow proper procedures regarding the duty to report all suspected incidents of child abuse, including molestation. Most administrators have faced the problem of having to deal with charges of molestation in the school. If they have yet to experience the problem, the probability is that they know of a colleague who has.

The bottom line is this: Charges of molestation are serious and must be handled in accordance with established board policy and the law.

Questions for Reflection

What does board policy stipulate regarding ways in which charges of molestation must be handled in the school? What steps has the administrator of my school taken to assure that all concerned understand and abide by policy and the law governing reporting of child molestation? Have the policies of our school been reviewed by legal counsel to assure they comply with state law? What insights, concerns, or questions do you have regarding this statement?

Successful Leaders Focus on Quality, Equity, and Caring

A learning-centered leader knows that successfully educating children requires a sustained collaborative effort on the part of the board of education, community, faculty, staff, and administration. Assuring that all children reach a high level of academic achievement in made possible when the leadership remains focused on quality education, equity, and caring. Successful educational leaders lead the school/community stakeholders in the development of a clear mission and goals to serve as guide for the education of children. They lead the development of a positive environment for teaching and learning, in which a safe harbor exists for the free exchange of ideas regarding what is required to successfully educate all children to live a lifetime of success as adults. Learning-centered leaders know that school boards, community, faculty, staff, administration, and students will stay clearly focused on accomplishing important education goals and high student achievement for all only to the degree that the leadership demonstrates that success for all is their primary concern. Learning-centered leaders produce the best results by practicing the following principles: The primary goal of successful educational leadership is high academic achievement for every student. Achieving this lofty goal result from educators taking genuine pride in the academic growth of all children. Leaders, educators, and children must be able to experience feelings of accomplishment and joy in their work. *Note*: Fear of failure must be expunged from the school environment. The mistaken beliefs that fear and sanctions represent effective motivation for either children or adults is wrong-headed thinking. Successful leaders promote quality, equity, and caring for all children, faculty, and staff.

Questions for Reflection

To what extent is the leadership in your school focused on academic achievement for all students? To what extent are fear of failure and sanctions used to motivate students, faculty, staff, and administrators? Does my school use high-stakes testing to measure academic achievement? What plan is in place to accommodate the wide variety of learning needs that predominate in my school? To what extent is the leadership of my school concerned with quality, equity, and care for students, faculty, and staff? What insights, concerns, or questions do you have regarding this statement?

The Case Against High-Stakes Testing

The current school reform movement relies too heavily on a high-stakes testing approach as a way to improve the quality of education in our schools. The drive for more accountability, as evidenced by high test scores, has caused state and national decision makers to ignore many of the more critical factors that must be provided to produce quality educational programs and services. Policy makers and school administrators should know that quality education comes from providing children with well-qualified teachers, a good curriculum, competent leadership, adequate supplies, books, laboratories, and other necessary school facilities.

They must also understand this reality: Quality education has never come from testing, nor will it ever. One need to look no further than the current school reform movement to see the failure associated with trying to produce better student achievement by using high-stakes testing to judge the quality of education.

Learner-centered leaders know that teachers, administrators, staff, and students must be allowed to succeed in their respective roles by demonstrating more concern for the individual dignity of all. Emphasis must be placed on teaching and learning. Students must be given the resources and time needed to master the knowledge, skills, and dispositions required to achieve academic success. Testing must be relegated to its only legitimate use: To discover what a child knows and what he/she needs to learn to achieve academic competency. When this goal is reached, the standardized test scores that state and national policy makers' demand might well be achieved. Continued misuse of high-stakes testing will most certainly render that outcome impossible. And for good reasons: State and federal policy makers have a shortsighted view of what constitutes a quality education. They lack the necessary understanding and knowledge of the complex process of educating children. They want excellence in education, but they don't have a clue regarding what constitutes a quality education. Unfortunately, too many of them believe that a fear of failure will motivate educators, parents, and students to do a better job. Nothing could be further from the truth. Fear of failure and severe sanctions over the long term can only serve to interfere with, impede, and ultimately arrest learning.

Questions for Reflection

How are high-stakes tests used to evaluate the success of children in my school? To what extent ate they used to measure the performance of the administration, faculty, staff, and school? How does high-stakes testing impact the curriculum in my school? How much time do teachers and students spend in preparing for testing in my school? What do teachers, parents, and students think about the value of high-stakes testing in my school? What insights, concerns, or questions do you have regarding this statement?

The Power of Parent Involvement

Studies regarding student success in school continue to validate the importance of parental involvement in the education of their children. Research demonstrates that academic achievement is more closely correlated with parent involvement than with economic status, race, or peer pressure. Parental involvement also proves to be beneficial to all ethnic groups. Also, active participation by either fathers or mothers has been found to equally benefit both boys and girls. Additionally, research shows that nearly all adolescents, whether living with birth parents, a parent, and a step-parent, or a single parent, do better in school when a parent or guardian is involved. Simply put, children whose parents or guardians are involved in their education all experience a powerful academic benefit. Further, less educated mothers and fathers who take an active part in the education of their children appear to exert a greater influence on the academic success of their children than do their more educated counterparts. Significantly, high-risk students may benefit most from parental involvement in their education. The bottom line is: Research findings on parental involvement and academic achievement makes getting parents involved in the education of their children a top priority for school leaders.

Questions for Reflection

Does my school have a plan to get parents involved in the education of their children? What evidence exists to validate the extent of parental involvement in my school? Does the mission of my school clearly address parent involvement in the education of their children? What ideas, concerns, or questions do you have regarding this statement?

A Quality Education for All Children

School leaders must make providing all children with a quality education their top priority. Every decision they make must be in the best interest of children and their education. Special interest politics have no place in schools. The governing board, administration, faculty, and staff simply can't be the first concern of school leaders if children are to receive the high-quality education they deserve. School leaders who don't follow this fundamental principle are sure to fail.

Questions for Reflection

What ideas, concerns, or questions do you have regarding this statement?

Leading Requires Knowing and Taking Charge

Education leaders who think they lack sufficient power and authority to effectively lead their schools simply can't achieve success. Unfortunately, an increasing number of education leaders claim that the task of leading a school is becoming impossible. They point to new state and federal mandates and accountability rules, which they think infringes on their authority. There is little question that current school reforms have narrowed the scope of a school leaders authority to determine curriculum content, achievement outcomes, assessment strategies, and other school-related matters previously left to the judgment local school leaders and their faculty and staff. In addition, union contracts, political action groups, and overly involved parents and school boards have combined to impinge on the authority of local school leaders. In spite of these new impediments, school leaders continue to have sufficient authority to lead their schools. Learning more about leadership theory and the appropriate application of leadership skills can greatly enhance school leaders' ability to lead. Put bluntly, successful school leadership begins with knowing how to lead and then doing it. Taking charge of leading the school involves learning how to assert power and authority in positive ways. The following leadership principles employed professionally and consistently will result in greater power and authority.

- School leaders must be committed to exercising good leadership skills. They must be persistent in working on problems until they are settled. During the process of solving problems, school leaders must demonstrate effective listening skills. They must be able to identify the significant issues associated with problems, focus on important data, and carefully evaluate alternative solutions to problems.

- School leaders must be proactive and not allow events to drive them toward unsatisfactory solutions. Taking charge of a problem early on gives school leaders with more respect and influence.

- They must be decisive and demonstrate readiness to make tough decisions in timely ways.

- They must be courageous—not afraid to take a thoughtful risk—grounded on the best information available at the time.

- School leaders must demonstrate flexibility and show others that they are receptive to different points of view. People are more willing to follow leaders who are willing to consider new concepts, ideas, and perceptions.

- They must show respect, concern, and care for others.

- School leaders must demonstrate that they value the skills and talents that people possess, because these attributes are necessary to develop real solutions to difficult problems.

- School leaders know how to exercise appropriate political behavior. They must promote effective links between community agencies and stakeholders that must be dealt with. And, they must know who can best accomplish what, how, and at what expense.

- They must work all community stakeholders to establish the school policy and level of authority and control necessary to effectively lead the school.

- They must empower their faculty and staff. Effective delegation of authority to school staff, at appropriate levels, to make timely decisions a necessary is part of successful leadership.

- School leaders must know the history and current purpose of education. Being knowledgeable enables them to anticipate new educational needs, which will require attention.

Finally, school leaders must remain teachable, that is, they must know when and how to adjust their behavior, to seek input and advise from others, and perhaps—hardest of all—admit their mistakes. The bottom line is this: Effective school leaders know how to take charge of leading their respective schools. They know how to assert the legitimate power and authority they have been entrusted with to provide children with a quality education.

Questions for Reflection

How are power and authority exercised in my school? Do the leaders in my school assert authority constructively? Am I a take-charge leader? How would others describe my leadership style (aggressive of passive)? What are your perceptions, ideas, or concerns regarding this position statement?

Self-Control: A Leadership Perquisite

Effective leaders know the important role self-control plays in their success. Exercising self-control, especially when being attacked personally because of an opinion, or idea they have expressed is perquisite to successful leadership. Effective leaders know they simply can't lash out at those criticizing them. By maintaining self-control, leaders enhance their ability to work through conflict, in order to shed greater light on any problems they may be having and craft workable solutions. Leaders who strictly adhere to rules of good behavior are able to develop unfailing self-control and thus handle very difficult problems successfully and professionally.

Questions for Reflection

How well do the leaders in my school maintain self-control in my school? How well do I? Is self-control a matter our school leaders discuss? What ideas, concerns, or questions do you have regarding this statement?

Leaders Can't Know All

Effective leaders communicate well with all concerned. They accomplish this outcome, in part, by making sure they don't let their ego get in the way. For example, they understand that no one person can know everything. So, they don't try to be know-it-alls. In fact, one of the surest ways for leaders to lose respect and credibility is to behave as though they know something when they don't. Leaders who try to bluff their way through a discussion will lose the trust and confidence they must have to successfully lead others. Leaders are more successful when they are honest and candid in their communications with others. Make no mistake about it: It's always best to say, "I don't know the answer, but I will research the question and let you know," than it is to pretend you know something when you don't.

Questions for Reflection

How candid is the communication between the leadership and others in my school? How candid am I? Do sometimes try to bluff my way through an issue by pretending to know something? What would my peers say? What are your thoughts, or questions regarding this topic?

Improving Communication

Good communication begins with knowing that we might be wrong and others might not accept our ideas. Communication is enhanced when leaders refrain from finding fault with the ideas or thoughts of others. A suggested solution might not be the best alternative available, but effective leaders don't label the idea as faulty. They show respect for the person and the idea by building on the solution presented and continuing to invite additional ideas, alternatives and solutions. Proceeding in this way encourages all concerned to participate in the discussions at hand. Leaders must never permit themselves to become angry or feel bad when others do not favor ideas different than their own. Leaders who adopt this type of attitude encourage others to participate more fully in discussions and problem-solving sessions. They communicate better and thus are better able to lead others toward reaching agreement on what needs to be accomplished. Communication is improved and enhanced when leaders make sure others understand this reality: There are no sides to take when resolving problems—only goals to achieve.

Questions for Reflection

How open is the leadership in (my school) to the ideas and opinions of others? How open am I to the ideas and thoughts of others? How might our communications be improved in my school? What are your ideas, perceptions, or questions regarding this statement?

Communicating under Stressful Conditions

Leaders must take care to refrain from being overly critical of others when communicating in stressful circumstances, especially when emotions run high. When this happens, it's useful to remember that we might be wrong, that the perceptions of others may be more valuable than our own, be sure to show readiness to consider the ideas of others, be committed to working to reach consensus, and keep calm, listen carefully to what others have to say. Leading in this manner enhances the probability that we will be able to find solutions to difficult problems and at the same time find that others appreciate our leadership ability.

Questions for Reflection

How effective do the leaders in my school communicate during stressful times? How well do I? What could we do to improve communications in my school? What questions, ideas or concerns do you have regarding this statement?

3.5   Journal

"The brain does its best reflective work when provided with the time, place, and tools for the deliberate exercise of reasoning skills" (Dickmann & Stanford-Blair, 2002, p. 206).

Benefits of journaling have been identified as expanding awareness, understanding, and insights; making connections between theory and practice; and generating new hypotheses for action (Taggart & Wilson, 1998). The intern is strongly urged to use a journal.

It is best to write on a weekly basis, but is also advantageous to write immediately following significant insights, feelings, and/or experiences. Journaling assists the emerging leader in focusing on essential leadership skills and the results of his/her efforts. It is an opportunity for reflection. The time and thought used in journal writing reinforce the learning and assist in the leader's ability to truly begin reflection prior to and during action.

The intern should write entries for each of the planned activities and projects, as well as significant events during the school year. You may find that journal entries will help you in compiling your final report. Interns often keep journal entries in a separate file in the computer, whereas others prefer handwritten formats. The type of journal you keep is your choice.

3.6 Log

The intern must meet with the supervisor and agree on the method of documenting time and effort. Typically, logs should cite date, time (rounded off to the half-hour), and a brief statement describing the activity. An example:

9/05/03   1.0 hour   Observed Ms. Smith's classroom

3.7 Monitoring/Formative Evaluation

Plans almost always have to be changed. Typically, these changes occur as a result of

- ♦ Unexpected events
- ♦ New opportunities
- ♦ Suggestions/recommendations from mentors and/or interviewees
- ♦ New perspectives gained from experience and reflection
- ♦ Periodic formative evaluations

Any or all of the above can arise and cause the intern to adjust, add, and/or delete planned activities. The intern should determine and schedule periodic assessment of their progress and plan. The formative evaluation period should be monthly. It may be done on a regular schedule or as the need arises. The periodic evaluations, however, should be done on average once a month.

The formative evaluations should note progress toward completion of the plan and changes to the plan. Progress may be brief descriptions of how closely you are adhering to timelines and progressing in knowledge and skill. Changes should have a brief explanation of the circumstances and rationale for the change.

A summary of the formative evaluations, noting progress and changes will be presented at the final internship development experience report.

Stage Four

Internship Summative Evaluation

4.1 Summary and Evaluation of Experience

The intern is required to complete a summary and evaluation of experience for *each* of the 38 leadership areas. One summary and evaluation for each area is required, regardless of the amount of time or number of activities accomplished in the particular leadership area. The summary and evaluation of experience should be brief (one page or less) and include the following:

♦ Description of activity or activities in the area

♦ Significant knowledge attained and/or skill developed

♦ Additional knowledge and/or skill needed in the area

♦ Recommendations for school improvement in this area

♦ Personal beliefs/values concerning this area and motivation to lead in this area

4.2 Reflection on Action

Competence grows as one observes more. The goal is to observe more and have a greater range of models to draw from as the intern reflects on his/her own actions and the actions of others. The intern will summarize and provide highlights of his/her experience with reflective practice (see Sect. 3.3). Also include an overall *reflection on practice*, discussing the following:

♦ What models/concepts/theories were effective or not effective?

♦ What deep-seated beliefs guided your actions and experience?

♦ How did the history/traditions/culture of the district/school affect your actions?

127

♦ How did your emotional state/moods affect your actions and experience?

♦ How did the availability or lack of resources affect your actions?

♦ How did the on-the-job experience change your beliefs and actions?

4.3 School Improvement Lists

The intern will review all results obtained in the internship with regard to school improvement. The intern will compile a prioritized list of all *results* that led to school improvement. A second prioritized list will be compiled and submitted for *recommendations* for school improvement. The two lists should be developed from the direct internship, as opposed to general attitudes or prior thinking. The school improvement lists will be presented and submitted as part of the internship final report.

4.4 Developing Your Portfolio

Your portfolio is a compilation of relevant evidence of your knowledge, skill, and experience. It contains the best samples of your professional work and accomplishments. It may include degrees and certificates, but it is primarily evidence of the outcomes of your knowledge, skill, and experience. A professional portfolio should not be a scrapbook of training certificates, school papers, and notes from students.

Superintendent interns should review the State, ISLLC and AASA standards. Secondary principal interns should review the State and ISLLC standards and NASSP competencies. Elementary principal interns should review the State and ISLLC standards and NAESP proficiencies. It is recommended that you use these as your portfolio sections and provide *evidence* that you meet these standards.

At this point in your leadership development, it is understood that you may not have documentation or evidence of meeting all the standards. This is the beginning of your portfolio, however, and should serve to guide the planning of future professional development.

4.5 Vita Update

The intern should update his/her vita to include relevant accomplishments from the internship. This may be included in the leadership section of the vita for those not currently holding an administrative position. For experienced administrators, this is typically placed under the professional development category or administrative experience category. A copy of the updated vita should be presented at the final internship report.

4.6 Letter of Application

The letter of application should focus on the specific career goal of the intern. For example, if the intern wants the position of assistant superintendent for curriculum, the letter of application should be written for that position. If the intern would like an assistant principal position prior to applying for a principalship, the letter should be written for that position. In drafting the letter, the intern must assess his/her knowledge, disposition, skill, and the match to the position and district.

The letter of application will be the first impression you make of your career plans and experiences, and it explains how you may benefit the district. It should bring out the highlights of your vita and your knowledge of the district and position. It is an opportunity to explain and expand your vita with a sample of your writing, philosophy, and vision, and it should show how these conform to the needs and expectations of the district/school. The letter of application should have the following four sections:

Section 1—Intent of Letter

The first paragraph must begin with the purpose or intent of the letter. In this case, you should write that you are officially applying for the particular position. Next, you should include that you are aware of the duties and responsibilities of the position. (If you are not currently knowledgeable of this position, be sure to acquire this knowledge during your internship/professional development experience). Next, you should include a statement as to whether you meet all of the qualifications. If you do not, you should either specify which qualifications you do not meet or indicate how or when they will be met.

Some applicants include a personal bit of information in this section. This could be that you are excited about the possibility of assuming this position or that you have been preparing for this position, or whatever. If you decide to add a personal statement, be sure that it is honest and relevant.

Section 2—Your Half of the Match

This section includes the highlights of the knowledge, skill, and experience that you are bringing to the district. This is your offer to the district. This is what they will be getting. It is written with the intent of informing the district what you can offer them for the future versus what you accomplished for someone else in the past. An example of this is to state that you bring two years of experience in administering a primary reading program, instead of stating that you ran the Distar Program for the XYZ District. Although this is a subtle distinction, keep in mind that districts are looking for someone to belong and work for them, not an outsider.

This section is an opportunity to summarize your vita. For example, you can include the highest degree attained, total number of years in education, relevant training or experience, and the like. You can also provide further explanation and/or additional information not included in your vita. Examples include your background, types of students you have worked with, evaluations, successes with particular students, and other relevant information.

This section should also include your principles, beliefs, philosophy, and vision. The intent here is to provide a deeper understanding of your character and your style. Again, it needs to be future-oriented and relate to how you will demonstrate these qualities in your new position. Much time and thought should be used in preparing this section. Consider the key beliefs and the guiding principles that you will rely on in your new leadership position.

Section 3—Your Match with the District

Ideally, this section shows how your knowledge, skill, and experience meet the current and future needs of the district. This will require that you become knowledgeable of the history, current issues, and future demands of the district. The intern must do the work of gathering information about the district/school and the particular position sought. You must analyze the needs of the district and position, in light of your experience and abilities. This is your opportunity to show that you are the right match.

Section 4—Thankful and Bold Conclusion

This section concludes your letter of application. It should offer a thank-you for the time and effort the district took to review your application materials. It should also make a bold statement of your expectation of being hired or continuing in the hiring process. An example of this is to state that you look forward to the further discussion of your accepting this position. This is much more positive and bold than concluding with a hope of hearing from them. If you have accurately assessed yourself and the district and know that you will be successful in meeting the needs of the position, you deserve to be bold. As with the first paragraph of the letter of application, you may choose to add any other personal or relevant items to this section. Use your best judgment. A copy of the letter should be presented at the final internship/professional development experience report.

Application Letter Guidelines

- ◆ One to one-and-a-half pages in length
- ◆ Short, clear paragraphs
- ◆ Describes you, not your previous employer
- ◆ Outlines the realization of the district's goals, not your own
- ◆ Shows you have done your homework (know district/school and its needs)
- ◆ Is checked and rechecked—grammar, spelling, style, intent
- ◆ Is positive/void of anything negative (districts want positive leadership)
- ◆ Clearly describes YOU and gives the district the opportunity to assess the match

A sample application letter is presented in Appendix A2.

4.7 Future Professional Development Plan

The intern must prepare and submit a three-year professional development plan based on his or her internship. This plan should discuss:

- ◆ Progress toward meeting the ISLLC standards
- ◆ Successes and failures in the intern experience
- ◆ Reflections in and on action
- ◆ Self, peer, and superior evaluations
- ◆ Position and leadership goals

Typically, a professional development plan focuses on the priorities or greatest needs of the administrator. The plan must be clear, manageable, and include a means of evaluation.

A clear plan lists specific objectives. It should cite actions to be taken, as opposed to a vague or general intent to improve in a particular area. This could include specific courses, workshops, or books; working with a mentor; or a host of other experiences. The intern must research available resources to meet his/her objectives. Objectives may include skill development, reevaluating dispositions, or attaining new knowledge.

A plan that is manageable includes actions that can be accomplished in a reasonable amount of time. Typically, three to five objectives are included in a three-year plan. This allows the intern one to two years to receive the new information and use or practice the new knowledge, disposition, or skill. A timeline for each objective must be included.

The plan must cite the criteria used to judge whether the objective was met. Ideally, this would be an artifact or other evidence that could be included in the portfolio. The professional development plan will be submitted at the final internship report.

4.8 Internship Report

In this final activity, the intern will prepare and present an overall report. Typically, the intern will present to his/her supervisors, either as part of many reports by others or individually. The report must be a professional presentation, similar to reporting to the Board. Documentation should include the items listed below. Following each item is the section in the text where the item is found.

- Summary of Individual Knowledge and Skill Assessment (1.2)
- Summary of Disposition Assessment/Others (1.3, 1.4)
- Position and Leadership Goals (1.5)
- Summary of District/School Goals and/or Improvement Plan (1.6)
- Summary and Evaluation of Experience (4.1)
- Summary of Local Project(s) (2.4)
- Summary of Reflective Practice (4.2)
- School Improvement Lists (4.3)
- Updated Vita (4.5)
- Portfolio (Section 4.4)
- Letter of Application (4.6)
- Activities Notebook (2.6)
- Networking List (2.5)
- Professional Resources and Affiliations (2.1, #37)
- Three-Year Professional Development Plan (4.7)
- Journal (3.5)
- Log (3.6)

The presentation should use overheads or PowerPoint to show highlights of overall experience. The length of the report should be agreed upon with supervisors prior to the presentation.

Suggested Further Readings

Vision

Bennis, W. (2003). *On Becoming a Leader* (3rd ed.). Cambridge, MA: Perseus Books.

Conley, D. T., Dunlap, D. M., & Goldman, P. (Winter 1992). The "Vision Thing" and School Restructuring. *OSSC Report* 32: 1-8. Eugene, OR: School Study Council, ED 343 246.

Elmore, R. F., et al. (1996). *Restructuring in the Classroom: Teaching, Learning, and School Organization*. San Francisco: Jossey-Bass.

Heifitz, R. (1994). *Leadership Without Easy Answers*. Cambridge, MA: Harvard University Press.

Heifitz, R., & Linsky, M. (2002). *Leadership on the Line: Staying Alive Through the Dangers of Leading*. Boston: Harvard Business School Press.

Decision Making

Estler, S. (1988). Decision making. In Boyles, N. J. (Ed.). *Handbook of Research on Educational Administration*, pp. 305–319. New York: Longman.

Herbert, H. A. (1960). *The New Science of Management Decisions*. New York: Harper and Row.

Hoy, W. K., & Tarter, C. J. (1995). *Administrators Solving the Problems of Practice: Decision-making Concepts, Cases, and Consequences*. Boston: Allyn and Bacon.

Lashway, L. (1999). *Measuring Leadership*. ERIC/CEM Publication Code EMOMLG.

Mitchell, D. E., & Tucker, S. (February 1992). Leadership as a Way of Thinking. *Educational Leadership*, 49(5): 10–11, EJ 439 276.

Nutt, P. C. (1989). *Making Tough Decisions*. San Francisco: Jossey-Bass.

Snowden, P. E., & Gorton, R. A. (2002). *School Leadership & Administration* (6th ed). New York: McGraw Hill.

Tannenbaum, R., & Schmidt, W. H. (March/April 1958). How to Choose a Leadership Pattern. *Harvard Business Review*, 36: 95–101.

Communication

Amundson, K. (1993). *Speaking and Writing Skills for Educators.* Arlington, VA: American Association of School Administrators.

Bridges, E. M. (1994). *PBL Project–Write Right!* ERIC/CEM Publication Code EPRWRI.

Covey, S. R. (1990). *The seven habits of highly effective people.* New York: Simon and Schuster.

Geddes, D. S. (1995). Keys to Communication: A Handbook for School Success. In J. J. Herman, & J. L. Herman (Eds.), *Practicing Administrator's Leadership Series.* Thousand Oaks, CA: Corwin Press.

Gemmet, R. A. (1977). *A Monograph on Interpersonal Communications.* Redwood City, CA: San Mateo County Superintendent of Schools, ED 153 323.

Glaser, S., & Biglan, A. (1977). *Increase Your Confidence and Skill in Interpersonal Situations: Instructional Manual.* Portland, OR: Northwest Regional Educational Laboratory, ED 095 127.

Harkins, P. (1999). *Powerful Conversations: How High-Impact Leaders Communicate.* New York: McGraw-Hill.

Jung, C., et al. (1973). *Interpersonal communications: Participant materials and leader's manual.* Portland: OR: Northwest Regional Educational Laboratory, ED 095 127.

Lysaught, J. P. (Summer 1984). Toward a Comprehensive Theory of Communication: A Review of Selected Contributions. *Educational Administration Quarterly,* p 102.

Michel, G. J., et al. (February 1995). What Are the Principal's Skills in School Communications? Paper presented at the meeting of the Management Institute, SC: Hilton Head. *ERIC Report,* 17–21, ED 383–084.

Rowicki, M. A. (1999). *Communication Skills for Educational Administrators.* ERIC In-Process Abstract Guides: Non-Classroom Use, pp. 199–208, EA029982.

Seiler, W. J., et al. (1982). *Communication in Business and Professional Organizations, chapter 1.* Reading, MA: Addison-Wesley.

Snowden, P. E., & Gorton, R. A. (2002). *School Leadership & Administration,* (6th ed). New York: McGraw Hill.

St. John, W. D. (1970). A Guide to Effective Communication. *Personal and Organizational Communication Series. ERIC Report,* ED 057–464.

Talbert, J. V., & Beran, D. (1999). *Journal for a Just and Caring Education,* 5(4): pp. 430–439.

Vann, A. S. (November 1994). That Vision Thing. *Principal,* 74(2): pp. 25–26.

West, P. (March 1989). Electronic Mailboxes: Novel Phone Links Close Gaps Between Parents and Schools. *Education Week,* p. 1.

Conflict and Issue Resolution

Bittel, L. R., et al. (1992). *What Every Supervisor Should Know: The Complete Guide to Supervisory Management*. New York: McGraw-Hill.

Blase, J., et al. (1992). *Bringing Out The Best In Teachers: What Effective Principals Do*. Thousand Oaks, CA: Corwin Press.

Brounstein, M., et al. (1993). *Handling the Difficult Employee: A Practical Guide for Managers*. Menlo Park, CA: Crisp Publishing.

Cadwell, C. M. (1988). *New Employee Orientation: a Practical Guide for Supervisors*. Menlo Park, CA: Crisp Publishing.

Carroll, M. (1996). *Workplace Counselling: A Systematic Approach to Employee Care*. London: Sage Publishing.

Fisher, R. (1991). *Getting to Yes: Negotiating Without Giving In,* (2nd ed). Boston: Houghton Mifflin.

Heider, J. (1985). *The Tao of Leadership*. New York: Bantam Books.

Kaplan, V., et al. (1996). *The A-to-Z book of managing people*. Berkley Publishing Group.

Snowden, P. E., & Gorton, R. A. (2002). *School Leadership & Administration,* (6th ed). New York: McGraw Hill.

Motivation

Besculides, G. (February 1999). Caring for Ourselves. *School Administrator*, 56(2): 34–36.

Clark, K. E., & Clark, M. (1996). *Choosing to lead*. Greensboro, NC: Center for Creative Leadership.

Cooley, V., & Jianping, S. (1999). Who Will Lead? The Top 10 Factors That Influence Teachers into Moving into Administration. *NASSP Bulletin*, 83(606): 75–80.

Gardner, J. W. (1990). *On leadership*. New York: The Free Press.

Goleman, D., Boyatzis, R., & McKee, A. (2002). *Primal Leadership, Realizing the Power of Emotional Intelligence*. Boston: Harvard Business School Press.

Lashway, L. (1997). Visionary Leadership. *ERIC Digest*, (110). Eugene, OR: ERIC Clearinghouse on Educational Management,

Maccoby, M. (2001). *Why Work? Leading the New Generation*. Alexandria, VA: Miles River Press.

Maxwell, J. (1993). *Developing the Leader Within You*. Nashville: Thomas Nelson Publishing.

McDaniel, T. R. (April 1999). Discovering the "Inner Teacher": Concepts, Questions, and Caveats. *American Secondary Education*, 27(3): 31–35.

Snowden, P. E., & Gorton, R. A. (2002). *School Leadership & Administration,* (6th ed). New York: McGraw Hill.

Wendell, F. C., Schmidt, A. H., & Loch, J. (1992). *Measurements of Personality and Leadership: Some Relationships.* Lincoln, NE: University of Nebraska, ED 350 694.

Group Processes (and Consensus Building)

Amundson, K. (1993). *Speaking and writing skills for educators.* Arlington, VA: American Association of School Administrators.

Covey, S. R. (1990). *The seven habits of highly effective people.* New York: Simon and Schuster.

Geddes, D. S. (1995). Keys to Communication. A Handbook for School Success. In J. J. Herman, & J. L. Herman (Eds), *Herman Practicing Administrator's Leadership Series.* Thousand Oaks, CA: Corwin Press, ED 377–575.

Gron, P. C. (March 1983). Talk As They Work: The Accomplishment of School Administration. *Administrative Science Quarterly, 1–21.*

Ishmer, K. (1996). Communication Skills. *ERIC Digest,* 102.

Lysaught, J. P. (Summer 1984). Toward a Comprehensive Theory of Communication: A Review of Selected Contributions. *Educational Administration Quarterly,. 102.*

Michel, G. J., et al. (February 1995). *What are the principal's skills in school communications?* pp.17–21. A paper presented at the meeting of the Management Institute, SC: Hilton Head. *ERIC Report,* ED 383–084.

Osterman, K. F. (October 1993). *Communication Skills: A Key to Caring, Collaboration, and Change,* pp. 29–31. A paper presented at the annual conference of the University Council for Educational Administration, TX: Houston, ED 363 973.

Pierson, P. R., & Bredeson, P. V. (September 1993). It's Not Just a Laughing Matter: School Principals' Use of Humor in Interpersonal Communications with Teachers. *Journal of School Leadership,* 3(5): 522–33, EJ 466 909.

Richardson, L. M. (1998). Stress in the Superintendency: Implications for Achieving Excellence. *ERIC In-Process* Abstract, 143–150.

Rosenburg, M. (1999). *Non-violent communication: A language of compassion.* Encinitas, CA: Puddle Dancer Press.

Rowicki, M. A. (1999). Communication Skills for Educational Administrators. *ERIC In-Process* Abstract, Guides: Non-Classroom Use, 199–208, EA029982.

Seiler, W. J., et al. (1982). *Communication in business and professional organizations,* chapter 1. Reading, MA: Addison-Wesley.

Snowden, P. E., & Gorton, R. A. (2002). *School Leadership & Administration*, (6th ed). New York: McGraw Hill.

St. John, W. D. A Guide to Effective Communication. Personal and Organizational Communication Series, p.1. *ERIC Report*, ED 057–464.

Leadership Style and Power

Blasé, J. R., & Blasé, J. (1997). *Handbook of Instructional Leadership: How Principals Promote Teaching and Learning*. Thousand Oaks, CA: Corwin Press.

Firth, G. R. (1998). Governance of School Supervision. In G. R. Pajak, & E. F. Pajak (Eds.) *The Handbook of Research on School Supervision*. New York: Macmillion Library Reference.

Fritz, R. (1996). *Corporate tides: The inescapable laws of organizational structure*. San Francisco: Berrett-Koehler.

Goleman, D., Boyatzis, R., & McKee, A. (2002). *Primal leadership, realizing the power of emotional intelligence*. Boston: Harvard Business School Press.

Helslep, R. (1997). The Practical Value of Philosophical Thought for the Ethical Dimension of Educational Leadership. *Educational Administration Quarterly*, 33: 67–85.

Hong, L. K. (1996). *Surviving school reform: A year in the life of one school*. New York: Teachers College Press.

Lashway, L. (1997). Measuring Leadership Potential. *ERIC Digest*, 115.

Lashway, L., Mazzarella, J. A., & Grundy, T. (1997). Portrait of a Leader. In S. C. Smith & P. K. Piele (Eds.) *School Leadership: Handbook for Excellence*, (3rd ed). Eugene, OR: ERIC Clearinghouse on Educational Management.

Leithwood, K. A. (February 1992). The Move Toward Transformational Leadership. *Educational Leadership*, 49(5): 8–12, EJ 439 275.

Leithwood, K. A. & Jantzi, D. (June 1990). Transformational Leadership: How Principals can Help School Cultures. Paper presented at annual meeting of the Canadian Association for Curriculum Studies, British Columbia: Victoria, ED 323 622.

Liontos, L. B. (August 1992). Transformational Leadership. *ERIC Digest*, 72, ED 347 636.

Loup, K. S., & Cordeiro, P. A. (1997). The Implications of Partnerships for Preparation and Professional Growth of Educational Leaders. In R. Ackerman, & P. Cordeiro (Eds.) *Boundary Crossing: Educational Partnerships and School Leadership*. San Francisco: Jossey-Bass.

Mathews, D. (1996). *Is There a Public for Public School?* Dayton, OH: Kettering Foundation Press.

Poplin, M. S. (February 1992). The Leader's New Role: Looking to the Growth of Teachers. *Educational Leadership*, 49(5): 13–18, EJ 439 277.

Sagor, R. D. (February 1992). Three Principals Who Make a Difference. *Educational Leadership*, 49(5): 10–11, EJ 439 276.

Sergiovanni, T. J. (1994). *Building Community in Schools*. San Francisco: Jossey-Bass.

Schwahn, C. J., & Spady, W. G. (1998). *Total Leaders: Applying the Best Future-Focused Change Strategies to Education*. Arlington, VA: American Association of School Administrators.

Snowden, P. E., & Gorton, R.A. (2002). *School Leadership & Administration*, (6th ed). New York: McGraw Hill.

Starratt, R. J. (1995). *Leaders with Vision: The Quest for School Renewal*. Thousand Oaks, CA: Corwin Press.

Swan, W. W., & Brown, C. L. (Winter 1997). Collaborative Leadership—A Means to Build Unified Leadership. *The Reporter*, 22–23.

Van Velsor, E., & Leslie, J. B. (1991). *Feedback to Managers. Volume II: A Review and Comparison of Sixteen Multi-rater Feedback Instruments*. Greensboro, NC: Center for Creative Leadership, ED 351 391.

Wendel, F., Schmidt, A. H., & Loch, J. (1992). *Measurements of Personality and Leadership: Some Relationships*. Lincoln, NE: University of Nebraska, ED 350 694.

Whitaker, K. S., & Moses, M. C. (1994). *The Restructuring Handbook: A Guide to School Revitalization*. Boston: Allyn and Bacon.

Wincek, J. (1995). *Negotiating the Maze of School Reform: How Metaphor Shapes Culture in a New Magnet School*. New York: Teachers College Press.

Culture and Climate

Boyer, E. L. (September 1995). Making a Commitment to Character. *Principal*, 29.

Firestone, W. A., & Wilson, B.L. (Spring 1985). Using Bureaucratic and Cultural Linkages to Improve Instruction: The Principal's Contribution. *Educational Administration Quarterly*, 7–30.

Hallinger, P., Bickman, L., & Davis, K. (March 1989) What Makes a Difference? School Context, Principal Leadership, and Student Achievement. Paper presented at the Annual Meeting of the American Educational Research Association, San Francisco, CA, ED 332 341; ED 308 578.

Kohn, A. (May 1996). What's Wrong with Character Education. *ASCD Education Update*, 5.

Sergiovanni, T. J. (May 1990). Adding Value to Leadership Gets Extraordinary Results. *Educational Leadership*, 47(8): 23–27, EJ 410 204.

Snowden, P. E., & Gorton, R. A. (2002). *School Leadership & Administration*, (6th ed). New York: McGraw Hill.

Wegerif, R. (Autumn/Winter 1998). Two Images of Reason in Educational Theory. *The School Field,* 9(3–4): 77–105.

Change

Chenowith, T. G., & Everhart, R. B. (2002). *Negotiating Comprehensive School Change.* Larchmont, New York: Eye On Education.

Kotter, J. (2002). *The Heart of Change: Real-Life Stories of How People Change Their Organizations.* Boston: Harvard Business School Press.

Kotter, J. (1998). *Leading Change.* Cambridge: Boston Business School Press.

Fullan, M. (2001). *Leading in a Culture of Change.* San Francisco: Jossey-Bass.

Senge, P., et al. (1999) *The Dance of Change: The Challenges to Sustaining Momentum in Learning Organizations.* New York: Currency/Doubleday.

Evaluation–Instructional Evaluation

Angelo, T. A., et al. (October 1994). *Classroom Assessment Techniques: A Handbook for College Teachers,* (2nd ed). San Francisco: Jossey-Bass Publishers.

Astin, A. W. (December 1996). *Assessment for Excellence: The Philosophy and Practice of Assessment and Evaluation in Higher Education* (American Council on Education/Oryx Series). Phoenix, AZ: Oryx Press.

Gredler, M. (April 1994). *Designing and Evaluating Games and Simulations: A Process Approach.* Houston, TX: Gulf Publishing.

Kirkpatrick, D. L. (February 1996). *Evaluating Training Programs: The Four Levels.* San Francisco, CA: Berrett-Koehler.

Mager, R. F. (May 1997). *The Mager Six-Pack,* (3rd ed). Atlanta, GA: Center for Effective Performance.

Robinson, D. G., et al. (June 1989). *Training for Impact: How to Link Training to Business Needs and Measure the Results.* San Francisco: Jossey-Bass.

Walvoord, B. E., et al. (February 1998). *Effective Grading: A Tool for Learning and Assessment.* San Francisco: Jossey-Bass.

Wiggins, G. P., et al. (February 1998). *Educative Assessment: Designing Assessments to Inform and Improve Student Performance.* San Francisco: Jossey-Bass.

Worthen, B. R., et al. (December 1996). *Program Evaluation: Alternative Approaches and Practical Guidelines,* (2nd ed). Boston: Addison-Wesley.

Appendix A.1

Sample Vita

George Washington
1508 West 14th Street, Mount Vernon, AZ 50555
(W) (303) 555–7837 x322, (H) (303) 555–9069, gwash@used.org

Education/Certification

M.Ed.	Multicultural Education, Northern Arizona University, Flagstaff, AZ., 1998
B.A.	English, Carleton College, Northfield, MN, 1993
Principal Certificate	Arizona (in progress)
Teacher Certificate	7–12 English, Arizona and Minnesota
ESL Education	K–12 Endorsement, Arizona and Minnesota

Administrative and Leadership Experience

Assistant Principal, Martha High School, Vernon Union High School District, Vernon, AZ, 2000–present

- ♦ Administered campus activities including over 50 school clubs, school facility use, and school ceremonies
- ♦ Expanded the student recognition program designed to reward and promote student attendance, academic achievement, and responsible actions on campus
- ♦ Evaluated and provided guidance for a variety of teachers throughout the school using the district's evaluation instrument and informal observations and conferences

English Department Chairperson, Martha High School, Vernon, AZ 1999–2000

- Designed a department-based professional literacy library and conference center to help teachers better their pedagogical skills

- Implemented an English department collaborative teaching plan that promoted positive teacher communication regarding units and lessons, methodology, classroom management, and student achievement

- Planned and presented various English department in-services designed to improve classroom instruction, time management, and grant writing

- Evaluated all English teachers using the district's evaluation instrument and informal observations while carefully monitoring the progress of new and inexperienced teachers

North Central Accreditation Writing Goal Chairman, Martha High School, Vernon, AZ, 1999–present

- Designed and implemented an in-service program for teachers in all subject areas to ensure successful writing instruction across the curriculum

- Presented instructional methodology to assist all staff members in teaching and using the six-trait writing rubric, creating quality writing prompts, and paragraph and essay organization

Learning 24/7 Leadership Team Member, Martha High School, Vernon, AZ, 2000–present

- Advised and designed a school-wide plan to assure our students' success in the classroom, on standardized tests, and in life

- Aligned school curricula, incorporated test-taking skills into the curriculum, created a strong school-wide emphasis on basic reading, writing, and math skills in every class, and incorporated critical thinking skills across the curriculum

- Evaluated the specific instructional needs of our students and teachers by meticulously surveying and analyzing student test data, grades, and district assessments

Head Basketball Coach, Martha High School, Vernon, AZ, 1995–2000

- ◆ Incorporated a successful parent booster club that raised funds to support the basketball program
- ◆ Created a successful basketball program that won at least 19 games in each of the last three seasons while maintaining a team grade point average greater than a 3.2

Teaching Experience

High School English Teacher, Martha High School, Vernon, AZ, 1994–2000

- ◆ Integrated a variety of teaching methods and instructional strategies to generate student interest
- ◆ Evaluated and tracked student progress in class by using a combination of evaluations and student work samples
- ◆ Maintained positive relationship with students and parents while holding students to a high standard of acceptable class work

Upward Bound English Teacher, Normandale Upward Bound Program, Normandale Community College, Richfield, MN, 1994

- ◆ Designed a writing workshop for students involved to create, edit, and revise their own work in a summer writing portfolio
- ◆ Published a variety of works from every student's summer writing portfolio in a book distributed to all students and parents at the end of the summer

Coaching Experience

Head Basketball Coach, Martha High School, Vernon, AZ, 1995–2000

- ◆ Incorporated a successful parent booster club that raised funds to support the basketball program

♦ Created a successful basketball program that won at least 19 games in each of the last three seasons while maintaining a team grade point average greater than a 3.2

Additional Training/Professional Development

"Cutting Edge Grant Writing," Otter Creek Institute, Phoenix, AZ, May, 2000

"Increasing Student Achievement," National School Conference Institute, Phoenix, AZ, March, 2000

Presentations

Washington, G. (2000, September). *Improving Student Writing.* Presentation at the Inter-District Articulation Program, Yuma, AZ.

Washington, G. (2000, September). *Incorporating Writing in all Classrooms.* Presentation at the Martha High School Faculty Inservice, Vernon, AZ.

Washington, G. (2000, August). *Cibola's NCA Writing Goal and the Six-Trait Writing Rubric.* Presentation at the Martha High School Inservice Program, Vernon, AZ.

Professional Affiliations

Association for Supervision and Curriculum Development, 1999–present
National Association of Secondary School Principals, 2000–present
Arizona Professional Educators, 2000–present

References

References will be included on the following page, if requested.

Appendix A.2

Sara Teacher
555 Maple Avenue
Miami, FL 50001
(999) 555–2122

April 15, 2004

Jack Armstrong, Personnel Director
ABC School District
Fort Lauderdale, FL 50000

This letter is to officially apply for the position of Assistant Principal at Baywatch Elementary School. I am fully aware of the duties and responsibilities of the position. My education, teaching experience, and certification meet all of the posted requirements. After serious consideration, colleague support, and our administration advising that I apply, I am certain that I am ready and prepared to assume the duties of the Assistant Principal.

I bring to the position 12 years of successful teaching. This includes four years working with minority and poverty students, two years with gifted and talented, and eight years with numerous inclusive special education students. My students have performed better than the district and state average on tests and very few have needed administrative disciplinary assistance. I have formed excellent relationships with parents and members of the community. My successful teaching performance has allowed me to serve in many leadership capacities. I have served as grade-level Chair, Site Council representative, textbook committee Chair, math curriculum Chair, and sponsored numerous student organizations and school programs.

My administrative internship allowed me to gain experience in teacher observations, student discipline, budgeting and purchasing, staff development, and general office duties and responsibilities. I have taken an active part in special education reviews, expulsion hearings, hiring interviews, parent conferences, and the opening and ending school-year procedures. I understand the duties and operations of pupil and staff personnel, federal programs, transportation, athletics, and the curriculum department. I fully understand the role of the Assistant Principal and how to fulfill the needs of the various departments listed above.

I believe strongly in collaboration. This includes both the Principal and administrative staff and the faculty and students. I believe better decisions are made through participation and effective communication. I believe our first priority is student learning, whether academic or social. I believe in modeling fairness, openness, honesty, and always acting in an ethical manner. I believe what we do has a much greater impact on others than what we say. I believe in the goodness of everyone and that care and concern for others is the first step to reaching them and finding ways for them to achieve success.

I believe my knowledge, skill, and experience can greatly assist the ABC District in meeting its vision, mission, and goals. I know I will assist teachers in planning and implementing lessons, remediation, and effective evaluation techniques. I will provide the support and leadership that the teachers and staff expect and desire. I will treat them with the respect and professionalism that they deserve. I will continue to set high expectations for the faculty, the students, and myself. Although my main focus is on support, motivation, and preventative strategies, I am very firm with any individuals that are not meeting expectations. I will demand excellence, but will make every effort to coach and assist them to reach excellence.

I have thoroughly enjoyed teaching and look forward to offering my experience, dedication, and skills to the faculty of Baywatch Elementary. I look forward to learning from and working with the current Principal and fellow administrators. I appreciate your review of my letter, application, vita, and supporting documents. I look forward to discussing my role as Assistant Principal with you further. If any additional information is needed, please advise.

Respectfully,

Sara Teacher

Appendix A.3

American Association of School Administrators

Professional Standards for the Superintendency

Standard 1: Leadership and District Culture

1. Demonstrate executive leadership by developing a collective district vision

2. Shape school culture and climate.

3. Provide purpose and direction for individuals and groups.

4. Demonstrate an understanding of international issues affecting education.

5. Formulate strategic plans, goals, and change efforts with staff and community.

6. Set priorities in the context of community, student, and staff needs.

7. Serve as an articulate spokesperson for the welfare of all students in a multicultural context.

Standard 2: Policy and Governance

1. Develop procedures for working with the board of education that define mutual expectations, working relationships, and strategies for formulating district policy for external and internal programs.

2. Adjust local policy to state and federal requirements and constitutional provisions, standards, and regulatory applications.

3. Recognize and apply standards involving civil and criminal liabilities.

Standard 3: Communications and Community Relations

4. Articulate district purpose and priorities to the community and mass media.

5. Request and respond to community feedback.

6. Demonstrate consensus building and conflict mediation.

7. Identify, track, and deal with issues.

8. Formulate and carry out plans for internal and external communications.

9. Exhibit an understanding of school districts as political systems by applying communication skills to constituencies in support of district priorities.

10. Build coalitions to gain financial and programmatic support.

11. Formulate democratic strategies for referenda.

12. Relate political initiatives to the welfare of children.

Standard 4: Organizational Management

1. Exhibit an understanding of the school district as a system by defining processes for gathering, analyzing, and using data for decision making.

2. Manage the data flow.

3. Frame and solve problems.

4. Frame and develop priorities and formulate solutions.

5. Reach others to form reasoned opinions.

6. Reach logical conclusions and make quality decisions to meet internal and external customer expectations.

7. Plan and schedule personal and organization work.

8. Establish procedures to regulate activities and projects.

9. Delegate and empower at appropriate organizational levels.

10. Secure and allocate human and material resources.

11. Develop and manage the district budget.

12. Maintain accurate fiscal records.

Standard 5: Curriculum Planning and Development

1. Design curriculum and a strategic plan that enhance teaching and learning in multiple contexts.

2. Provide planning and future methods to anticipate occupational trends and their educational implications.

3. Identify taxonomies of instructional objectives and validation procedures for curricular units, using theories of cognitive development.

4. Align and sequence curriculum.

5. Use valid and reliable performance indicators and testing procedures to measure performance outcomes.

6. Describe the proper use of computers and other learning and information technologies.

Standard 6: Instructional Management

1. Exhibit knowledge of instructional management by implementing a system that includes research finding on learning and instructional strategies, instructional time, advanced electronic technologies, and resources to maximize student outcomes.

2. Describe and apply research and best practice on integrating curriculum and resources for multicultural sensitivity and assessment strategies to help all students achieve at high levels.

Standard 7: Human Resources Management

1. Develop a staff evaluation and development system to improve the performance of all staff members.

2. Select appropriate models for supervision based on adult motivation research.

3. Identify alternative employee benefits packages.

4. Describe and apply the legal requirements for personnel selection, development, retention, and dismissal.

Standard 8: Values and Ethics of Leadership

1. Understand and model appropriate value systems, ethics, and moral leadership.

2. Know the role of education in a democratic society.

3. Exhibit multicultural and ethnic understanding and related behavior.

4. Adapt educational programming to the needs of diverse constituencies.

5. Balance complex community demands in the best interest of the student.

6. Scan and monitor the environment for opportunities for staff and students.

7. Respond in an ethical and skillful way to the electronic and printed new media.

8. Coordinate social agencies and human services to help each student grow and develop as a caring informed citizen.

Appendix A.4

National Association of Secondary School Principals

Setting Instructional Direction

1. Implementing strategies for improving teaching and learning, including putting programs and improvement efforts into action

2. Developing a vision and establishing clear goals

3. Providing direction in achieving stated goals

4. Encouraging others to contribute to goal achievement

5. Securing commitment to a course of action from individuals and groups

Teamwork

1. Seeking and encouraging involvement of team members

2. Modeling and encouraging the behaviors that move the group to task completion

3. Supporting group accomplishment

Sensitivity

1. Perceiving the needs and concerns of others

2. Dealing tactfully with others in emotionally stressful situations or in conflict

3. Knowing what information to communicate and to whom

4. Relating to people of varying ethnic, cultural, and religious backgrounds

Resolving Complex Problems

Judgment

1. Reaching logical conclusions and making high quality decisions based on available information
2. Giving priority and caution to significant issues
3. Seeking out relevant data, facts, and impressions
4. Analyzing and interpreting complex information

Results Orientation

1. Assuming responsibility
2. Recognizing when a decision is required
3. Taking prompt action as issues emerge
4. Resolving short-term issues while balancing them against long-term objectives

Organizational Ability

1. Planning and scheduling one's own and the work of others so that resources are used appropriately
2. Scheduling flow of activities
3. Establishing procedures to monitor projects
4. Practicing time and task management
5. Knowing what to delegate and to whom

Communication

Oral Communication

1. Clearly communicating
2. Making oral presentations that are clear and easy to understand

Written Communication

1. Expressing ideas clearly in writing
2. Demonstrating technical proficiency
3. Writing appropriately for different audiences

Developing Self and Others

Development of Others

1. Teaching, coaching, and helping others
2. Providing specific feedback based on observations and data

Understanding Own Strengths and Weaknesses

1. Understanding personal strengths and weaknesses
2. Taking responsibility for improvement by actively pursuing developmental activities
3. Striving for continuous learning

Appendix A.5

National Association of Elementary School Principals

Proficiencies for Principals
3rd Edition

Decision Making

1. Can articulate and utilize a decision-making/problem-solving process

2. Can identify situations requiring alternative forms of decision making and use them

3. Can implement strategic planning decision making

4. Can understand and implement differing levels of involvement of others in the decision-making process.

5. Can utilize a method of evaluating decisions for learning and improvement

Communication

1. Can understand the communication process

2. Can implement strategies of gathering communication/information

3. Can implement strategies for monitoring communication

4. Can utilize effective strategies for sending communication/information

5. Can utilize effective listening skills

6. Can understand and utilize effective nonverbal communication strategies

7. Can utilize current technology in transmission of information

Leadership

1. Can articulate personal style of leadership

2. Can support leadership style from literature and experience

3. Can delegate and develop leadership in others

4. Can articulate vision for school and beyond

5. Can participate actively in local, state, and national professional associations

Group Processes

1. Can understand and use various group processes for goals, decisions, and evaluation including staff, parents, and students

2. Can articulate and use accepted decision-making model(s) in school settings

3. Can articulate and use consensus-building models

4. Can implement conflict resolution strategies with staff, parents, etc.

Problem Solving

1. Can understand and identify instances of role conflict

2. Can utilize an effective method for conflict resolution

3. Can implement practices that prevent major conflict

Educational Values and Culture

1. Can clearly state one's own philosophy and values in education and the school

2. Can identify values of others and the organization

3. Can be sensitive to differing values and culture while attaining goals of the school

School Improvement and Change

1. Can understand change and the change process
2. Can understand and identify resistance to change
3. Can implement strategies for facilitating change
4. Can use appropriate evaluation methods to guide change and improvement
5. Can utilize appropriate forms of needs assessments

Appendix A.6

Technology Standards for School Administrators

TSSA Draft Framework, Standards, and Performance Indicators (v4.0)

I. Leadership and Vision

Educational leaders inspire a shared vision for comprehensive integration of technology and foster an environment and culture conducive to the realization of that vision. Educational leaders:

A. Facilitate the shared development by all stakeholders of a vision for technology use and widely communicate that vision.

B. Maintain an inclusive and cohesive process to develop process to develop, implement, and monitor a dynamic, long-range, and systematic technology plan to achieve the vision.

C. Foster and nurture a culture of responsible risk-taking and advocate policies promoting continuous innovation with technology.

D. Use data in making leadership decisions

E. Advocate for research-based effective practices in use of technology

F. Advocate on the state and national levels for policies, programs, and funding opportunities that support implementation of the district technology plan.

II. Learning and Teaching

Educational leaders ensure that curricular design, instructional strategies, and learning environments integrate appropriate technologies to maximize learning and teaching.

Educational leaders:

A. Identify, use, evaluate, and promote appropriate technologies to enhance and support instruction and standards-based curriculum leading to high levels of student achievement.

B. Facilitate and support collaborative technology-enriched learning environments conducive to innovation for improving learning.

C. Provide for learner-centered environments that use technology to meet the individual and diverse needs of learners.

D. Facilitate the use of technologies to support and enhance instructional methods that develop higher-level thinking, decision-making, and problem-solving skills.

E. Provide for and ensure that faculty and staff take advantage of quality professional learning opportunities for improved learning and teaching with technology.

III. Productivity and Professional Practice

Educational leaders apply technology to enhance their professional practice and to increase their own productivity and that of others. Educational leaders:

A. Model the routine, intentional, and effective use of technology.

B. Employ technology for communication and collaboration among colleagues, staff, parents, students, and the larger community.

C. Create and participate in learning communities that stimulate, nurture, and support faculty and staff in using technology for improved productivity.

D. Engage in sustained, job-related professional learning using technology resources.

E. Maintain awareness of emerging technologies and their potential uses in education.

F. Use technology to advance organizational improvement.

IV. Support, Management, and Operations

Educational leaders ensure the integration of technology to support productive systems for learning and administration.

A. Develop, implement, and monitor policies and guidelines to ensure compatibility of technologies.

B. Implement and use integrated technology-based management and operations systems.

C. Allocate financial and human resources to ensure complete and sustained implementation of the technology plan.

D. Integrate strategic plans, technology plans, and other improvement plans and policies to align efforts and leverage resources.

E. Implement procedures to drive continuous improvement of technology systems and to support technology replacement cycles.

V. Assessment and Evaluation

Educational leaders use technology to plan and implement comprehensive systems of effective assessment and evaluation. Educational leaders:

A. Use multiple methods to assess and evaluate appropriate uses of technology resources for learning, communication, and productivity.

B. Use technology to collect and analyze data, interpret results, and communicate findings to improve instructional practices and student learning.

C. Assess staff knowledge, skills, and performance in using technology and use results to facilitate quality professional development and to inform personnel decisions.

D. Use technology to assess, evaluate, and manage administrative and operational systems.

IV. Social, Legal, and Ethical Issues

Educational leaders understand the social, legal, and ethical issues related to technology and model responsible decision-making related to these issues. Educational leaders:

A. Ensure equity of access to technology resources that enable and empower all learners and educators.

B. Identify, communicate, model, and enforce social, legal, and ethical practices to promote responsible use of technology.

C. Promote and enforce privacy, security, and online safety related to the use of technology.

D. Promote and enforce environmentally safe and healthy practices in the use of technology.

E. Participate in the development of policies that clearly enforce copyright law and assign ownership of intellectual property developed with district resources.

These standards are the property of the TSSA Collaborative and may not be altered without written permission. The following notice must accompany reproduction of these standards: "This material was originally produced as a project of the Technology Standards for School Administrators Collaborative."

Appendix A.7

Sample Case

"What Not to Wear"

Ted Smith was in his first year teaching 8th grade at Southwest Middle School. He had six years of previous teaching experience at another school with very good evaluations. He was popular with the students, but had little interaction with other teachers. He set high expectations, and his students scored higher that the district average on various normed and criteria-referenced tests. He appeared to enjoy teaching at Southwest and never voiced complaints.

In January, four other 8th grade teachers came to the principal's office with concerns about Mr. Smith's dress. The principal, Mrs. White, was surprised to see the teachers so upset and frustrated with the situation. They reported that they had observed Mr. Smith coming to school most days wearing jeans, T-shirts, and tennis shoes. They felt this was against policy that required "appropriate and professional dress." They wanted to know why the principal had allowed this to continue.

Mrs. White said that she knew Mr. Smith did not dress as nicely as most others, but that he had appeared to dress neatly and had never received any complaints before. The teachers remarked that they had heard complaints from many others and that his dress was unprofessional and embarrassing. They felt he was a poor model for the students and should not be given a new contract unless his dress met the policy. One of the teachers reminded the principal that she had made many comments about following policy during the year, but did not understand how Mr. Smith got away with not following policy.

Mrs. White said she would meet with Mr. Smith at the end of the day to discuss the matter.

Before reviewing the analysis on the following pages, what would you do?

It should be noted that in giving this case to many novice and experienced administrators, many simply said to call in Mr. Smith and inform him that his dress must improve and meet written policy—case closed, on to the next one. Consider whether the following analysis provides better information and leads to more appropriate actions than your initial reaction.

Vision (Shared Mission, Goals, Planning, Principles/Beliefs, Trust)

- Is there a clear vision of how the organization should be functioning now and in the future? Is it shared by all?
- Is the mission of the organization appropriate, understood, and supported?
- Has adequate planning occurred?
- Are the vision, mission, and plans aligned with the key principles and beliefs of those in the organization?
- Has trust been established between leadership, faculty, students, and community?
- What actions need to be taken to address any concerns from the above questions to solve the current problem and avoid similar problems in the future?

Aspects of the problem found:

No clear, shared vision on how the staff should dress

No shared understanding of the definition of "appropriate and professional"

Currently no plans to address professional dress

A sense of distrust by some teachers whether the principal enforces policy uniformly

Actions to be taken:

Choose a participatory or collaborative strategy to gather information or consensus on appropriate and professional dress.

Include an interpretation of the definition of appropriate dress in the Teacher Handbook.

Meet with or survey staff for other concerns in policy that the principal should address.

Follow up with the teachers to develop a higher degree of trust.

Decision Making

♦ Were the major steps in decision making followed?

- Need for a decision established
- Definition of the problem and gathering of information
- Identification of alternatives
- Assessment of alternatives
- Selection of best alternative
- Acceptance/support of decision
- Implementation of decision
- Evaluation of decision

♦ Was the appropriate decision making model used?

- *Rational/Scientific (classical)*—use of major steps to find one best solution; used for narrow, simple problems with complete information and certain outcomes

- *Satisficing*—use of major steps to find consensus (all satisfied) on solution; used with complex problems with partial information, uncertainty, but with definable satisfactory outcomes and adequate time for deliberation

- *Incremental*—choosing several alternatives and comparing results until agreement on course of action; used with incomplete information, complex problems, outcomes uncertain, no guiding policy, and general organizational chaos

- *Mixed Scanning*—same as incremental, but alternatives must be aligned with mission and philosophy; used with incomplete information, complex problems, outcomes uncertain, but a guiding policy and mission.

- *Garbage Can*—use of a previous solution to fit the current problem or no problem; used when dissatisfaction is present and solution is attractive

♦ Were those affected by the decision included in the process?

♦ What actions need to be taken to address any concerns from the above questions to solve the current problem and avoid similar problems in the future?

Aspects of the problem found:

No clear knowledge on the extent/magnitude of the problem. Are other teachers concerned? Are there others besides Mr. Smith that are not meeting policy?

No generation of alternatives to deal with Mr. Smith.

What decision model should be used?

How many should be involved?

Actions to be taken:

Meet with members of diverse formal and informal groups to ascertain the extent and magnitude of the problem.

Because staff has a high level of interest, and expertise on dress and buy-in are needed, use the satisficing model and seek a consensus through collaboration.

Because this affects all staff, include all staff in the collaboration.

Provide adequate time for staff to reach consensus.

Communication

- ◆ Has the leader been an effective giver of information? Both oral and written?
- ◆ Has the leader been an effective receiver of information?
- ◆ Has the leader been a good seeker of information? Are processes in place to gather information from all members of the organization with various formats?
- ◆ Has the leader monitored the communication aspects listed above?
- ◆ Is an effective two-way communication occurring at all times?
- ◆ What actions need to be taken to address any concerns from the above questions to solve the current problem and avoid similar problems in the future?

Aspects of the problem found:

The policy lacks needed detail, or the leader has not clarified the policy enough for all to understand.

This concern has bothered staff for many months and was not voiced before—why?

What other concerns are present and not reported to the principal?

There is a lack of agreement/understanding on the policy between the principal and staff.

Actions to be taken:

Ensure adequate detail is provided with the policy.

Communicate both orally and in writing the expectations for staff dress.

Take steps to inform staff of your desire and expectation to receive concerns.

Provide various avenues for soliciting concerns; that is, meet with departments on a regular basis, take time to mingle with staff and students before and after school and between periods, and promote an open-door policy and/or e-mail to you.

Assess the level of communication between yourself and staff, and seek a better network, if the current practice is not at an optimal level.

Conflict (Role, Values, and Issues)

♦ Do all persons within the organization understand the duties and responsibilities of their position and the positions of others?

♦ Are expectations for others realistic and aligned with job descriptions?

♦ Is conflict seen as an opportunity?

♦ Have steps been taken to resolve personal conflict and/or issue conflict? Have steps moved both sides toward a different and better solution (versus defensive argument of current positions)?

♦ What actions need to be taken to address any concerns from the above questions to solve the current problem and avoid similar problems in the future?

Aspects of the problem found:

Misunderstanding of the role of the principal and role of teachers in addressing an issue of policy.

No clear expectation on how teachers should voice concerns.

The teachers view the issue as embarrassing, not an opportunity for improvement.

No steps taken to resolve conflict between teachers.

Is there a better solution than simply directing Mr. Smith to dress more professionally?

What practices can be put into place to keep similar incidences from occurring?

Actions to be taken:

Clarify and communicate the role of the principal and teacher in issues of policy.

Elaborate to staff your desire to hear concerns and address concerns for improvements to the school and each of its members.

Provide staff development for conflict resolution at the personal and department level.

Gather as many alternatives as possible before making a decision.

Model conflict resolution for staff.

Motivation

- ♦ Are the needs of the people being met?
- ♦ Are the needs of the people in line with the needs or the organization?
- ♦ What processes are used to motivate? Are they effective?
- ♦ What actions need to be taken to address any concerns from the above questions to solve the current problem and avoid similar problems in the future?

Aspects of the problem found:

The needs of the 8th grade teachers are not being met.

Mr. Smith's needs are not in line with the organizational needs.

Mr. Smith does not appear to belong to any groups of faculty.

Consider a mentor or buddy system for new teachers.

Actions to be taken:

Use the satisficing model and seek consensus to ensure needs are met and aligned with the organizations needs and expectations.

Plan for all staff to be part of formal or informal groups.

Group Processes
(Consensus Building, Diversity, Coherence)

+ Have the formal and informal groups been identified?

+ Are all groups working productively and collaboratively?

+ Are goals for the groups realistic, understood, and acceptable?

+ Is trust and freedom of expression the norm of all groups?

+ Are meetings used effectively and efficiently?

+ What actions need to be taken to address any concerns from the above questions to solve the current problem and avoid similar problems in the future?

Aspects of the problem found:

Is Mr. Smith in an informal group? If not, why?

Does Mr. Smith participate in the formal 8th grade group? If not, why?

Does the 8th grade faculty have professionalism as one of its goals?

The 8th grade teachers have not developed trust and openness to discuss concerns.

How often does the 8th grade faculty meet? Are their meetings run effectively?

Have the 8th grade teachers been trained in leading and being a member of a group?

Actions to be taken:

Meet with Mr. Smith and discuss communication and collaboration with other 8th grade teachers and staff.

Provide training for the grade-level or department chair on leading meetings and others on being effective members of a group. Set an expectation for mutual trust.

Review meetings, agenda topics, and goals of the chair. Evaluate the importance and relevance.

Leadership Style, Power, Authority, and Influence

+ Has the appropriate style been used in this particular situation and with particular groups of people?

- *Directive (authoritarian, commanding)*—legal mandate; very little time, interest, and/or expertise of the followers; low need for quality and/or support for decision; higher need for task than people

- *Participative (democratic, input into decisions)*—limited time, limited expertise of leader, limited interest and/or expertise of followers, some degree of quality and support needed

- *Collaborative (democratic, shared decision making)*—adequate time available; high degree of interest and expertise of followers; high need for quality and support; desire for developing followers

- *Coaching*—adequate time; need to increase interest and expertise of followers; desire to develop followers and future leaders; need for support and assistance to individuals; higher need for people than task

- *Affiliative*—total concern for needs of people versus task

- *Laissez-Faire*—adequate time; high degree of interest and expertise of followers; low level of interest and/or expertise of leader; low need for quality of decision; desire to let others lead

♦ Has the appropriate power been used?

- *Reward*—recommended on a limited basis, never for political gain

- *Coercive*—recommended only in emergency situations, usually negative results

- *Expert*—used when leader has high degree of expertise over followers

- *Legitimate (position, legal authority)*—used to fulfill requirements of position

- *Referent*—used for consensus building and support

♦ What actions need to be taken to address any concerns from the above questions to solve the current problem and avoid similar problems in the future?

Aspects of the problem found:

Which style and power to use in resolving this matter?

Actions to be taken:

Decide on whether participative or collaborative style is needed. Directive in future violations of agreed upon policy interpretations.

Use the legitimate power of the position to carry out duties of position. Strive for additional referent (shared beliefs, values) power and/or expert power in communications, decisions, and group processes.

Culture (Values, Group Norms/ Processes, History) and Climate (Feelings)

♦ Are there issues of conflict/concerns with the current organizational culture?

♦ If so, has adequate time and resources been allocated in developing a new culture?

♦ Are there concerns with the current climate?

♦ Have adequate assessments been conducted to accurately assess the climate?

♦ What actions need to be taken to address any concerns from the above questions to solve the current problem and avoid similar problems in the future?

Aspects of the problem found:

Concerns of a needed culture of open communications

Concerns for a culture of professionalism in dress

At present no time nor resources given to this issue

Climate of frustration and ill feeling among some 8th grade teachers

No assessments on climate available or scheduled

Actions to be taken:

Meet with faculty and faculty groups and communicate your desire and the necessity for open communication.

Meet and find consensus on desires for and interpretations of professional dress.

Plan for time and resources for the above to happen.

Take extra time and effort in meeting the needs of the concerned 8th grade teachers.

Plan periodic assessments of school climate and take measures to address any concerns.

Change

- ♦ Is there a moral purpose in the new change?
- ♦ Do all involved understand the change process?
- ♦ Have positive relationships been built?
- ♦ Is the creation and sharing of information a priority?
- ♦ Has a productive disturbance and a subsequent coherence been accomplished?
- ♦ What actions need to be taken to address any concerns from the above questions to solve the current problem and avoid similar problems in the future?

Aspects of the problem found:

Actions to be taken:

No major change efforts planned

Evaluation (Monitoring, Assessments, New Cycle)

- ♦ Are effective personnel and program evaluations established?
- ♦ Are both formative and summative evaluation utilized?
- ♦ Are data from evaluations used for decisions and planning?
- ♦ What actions need to be taken to address any concerns from the above questions to solve the current problem and avoid similar problems in the future?

Aspects of the problem found:

Adequate information on dress not part of hiring or induction practices

Periodic assessments of climate, concerns, and needs not used

Actions to be taken:

Review hiring information and ensure issues of professional dress are included.

Develop and use assessments at the beginning, middle, and end of the year to include measurements on climate, communication, and any others issues deemed important to staff and students.

Summary Comments

It should be noted that not all aspects of the problem have surfaced at this time. Also, many of the areas of analysis overlap with others. For example, improper style, decision making, or communication can cause conflict and/or decrease motivation. Each area affects the other areas. Thus, there is overlap in defining the problem and considering actions to take. The intern must summarize and prioritize data collected from the analysis and then plan appropriate action.

References

Alderfer, C. (1972). *Existence, Relatedness, and Growth*. New York: Free Press.

Allison, D., & Allison, P. (1993). Trees and Forests: Details, Abstraction, and Experience in Problem Solving. In P. Hallinger, K. Leithwood, & J. Murphy (Eds.), *Cognitive Perspectives on Educational Leadership* (pp. 130–145). New York: Teachers College Press.

American Association of Colleges for Teacher Education (1988). *School Leadership: A Preface to Action*. Washington, DC: Author.

American Association of School Administrators (1960). *Professional Administrators for America's Schools (38th AASA Yearbook)*. Washington, DC: National Educational Administration.

American Association of School Administrators (1983). *Guidelines for the Preparation of School Administrators*. Arlington, VA: Author

American Association of School Administrators (1993). *Professional Standards for the Superintendency*. Arlington, VA: Author.

Ames, C. (1992). Classrooms: Goals, Structures, and Student Motivation. *Journal of Educational Psychology, 84*(3), 261–271.

Bandura, A. (1986*). Social Foundations of Thought and Action: A Social-Cognitive Theory*. Upper Saddle River, NJ: Prentice Hall.

Barnard, C. I. (1938). *Functions of an Executive*. Cambridge, MA: Harvard University Press.

Barth, R. S. (1990). *Improving Schools from Within*. San Francisco: Jossey-Bass.

Bennis, Warren. (2000). *Managing the Dream*. Cambridge, MA: Perseus.

Bennis, Warren. (1989). *On Becoming a Leader*. Reading, MA: Addison Wesley.

Bennis, W., & Nanus, B. (1985). *Leadership: The Strategies for Taking Charge*. New York: Harper & Row.

Bransford, J. D., Brown, A. L., Cocking, R. R. (2000). *How People Learn: Brain, Mind, Experience, and School: Expanded Edition*. Committee on Developments in the science of Learning with additional material from the Committee on Learning Research and Educational Practice, National Research Council. Washington, DC: National Academy Press.

Cameron, J., & Pierce, W. (1997). Rewards, Interest, and Performance: An Evaluation of Experimental Findings. *American Compensation Association Journal, 6*(4), 9–31.

Carnegie, D. (1993). *The Leader in You*. New York: Simon & Schuster.

Cohen, M. D., March, J. D., & Olsen, J. P. (1972). A Garbage Can Model of Organizational Choice. *Administrative Science Quarterly, 17*, 1–25.

Covey, S. R. (1989). *The Seven Habits of Highly Effective People*. New York: Simon & Schuster.

Dewey, J. (1938). *Logic: The Theory of Inquiry*. Troy, MO: Holt, Rinehart, & Winston.

Dickmann, M. H., & Stanford-Blair, N. (2002). *Connecting Leadership to the Brain*. Thousand Oaks, CA: Corwin.

Dunn, R., & Dunn, K. (1977). *Administrator's Guide to New Programs for Faculty Management and Evaluation*. Englewood Cliffs, NJ: Prentice Hall.

Erickson, D. A. (1981, December). *A New Strategy for School Improvement*. Momentum.

Etzioni, A. (1967). Mixed Scanning: A Third Approach to Decision Making. *Public Administration Review, 27*, 385–92.

Evans, Robert. (1996). *The Human Side of School Change*. San Francisco: Jossey-Bass.

Festinger, L. (1957). *A Theory of Cognitive Dissonance*. Evanston, IL: Row & Peterson.

Forsyth, P. B. (November, 1998). The School Administrator Supply. *Summary of the Denver Symposium*. National Policy Board of Educational Administration.

French, J. R., & Raven, B. (1959). The Bases for Social Power. In Darwin Cartwright (Ed.), *Studies of Social Power*, Ann Arbor: University of Michigan Press.

Fullan, M. (2002). *Leading in a Culture of Change*. New York: Wiley.

Fullan, M. (2001). *The New Meaning of Educational Change* (3rd ed.). New York: Teachers College Press.

Gardner, J. D. (1990). *On Leadership*. New York: Free Press.

Getzels, J. W. (1958). Administration as a Social Process. In Andrew Halpin (Ed.), *Administration Theory in Education*. Chicago: University of Chicago Midwest Administration Center.

Glasser, W. (1985). *Control Theory in the Classroom*. New York: Harper & Row.

Glidewell, J. (1993). How CEO's Change Their Mind. In P. Hallinger, K. Leithwood, & J. Murphy (Eds.), *Cognitive Perspectives on Educational Leadership* (pp. 34–53). New York: Teachers College Press.

Goleman, D. (2000, March-April). Leadership That Gets Results. *Harvard Business Review*, 78–90.

Goleman, D., Boyatzis, R., & McKee, A. (2002). *Primal Leadership, Realizing the Power of Emotional Intelligence*. Boston: Harvard Business School Press.

Gorton, R. A., & Snowden, P. E. (2002). *School Leadership and Administration* (6th ed.). New York: McGraw-Hill, p 31.

Greenberg, J., & Baron, R. A. (1997). *Behavior in Orgnizations*, (6th ed). Englewood Cliffs, NJ: Prentice Hall.

Guarino, S. (1974). *Communication for Supervisors*. Columbus: Ohio State University, p. 1.

Hallinger, P., Leithwood, K., & Murphy, J. (Eds.). (1993). *Cognitive Perspectives On Educational Leadership*. New York: Teachers College Press.

Hall, G. E., & Hord, S. M. (2001), *Implementing Change: Patterns, Principles, and Potholes*. Boston: Allyn and Bacon.

Heintzman, M., Leathers, D. G., Parrot, R. L., & Cairns, A. B. (1993). Nonverbal Rapport-Building Behaviors' Effects on Perception of a Supervisor. *Management Communication Quarterly, 7*(2), 181–208.

Hendricks, Gay, & Ludeman, Kate. (1996). *The Corporate Mystic: A Guidebook for Visionaries with their Feet on the Ground*. New York: Bantam.

Herzberg, F., Mauser, B., & Snyderman, B. (1959). *The Motivation to Work*. New York: Wiley.

Hoy, W. K., & Miskel, C. G. (2001). *Educational Administration: Theory, Research, and Practice* (6th ed.). New York: McGraw-Hill.

Hoyle, J., English, F. W., & Steffy, B. E. (1990). *Skills for Successful School Leaders* (2nd ed.). Arlington, VA: American Association of School Administrators.

Hoyle, J., English, F. W., & Steffy, B. E. (1998). *Skills for Successful 21st Century School Leaders*. Arlington, VA: American Association of School Administrators.

Jacobson, S. L. (July, 1996). School Leadership in an Age of Reform: New Directions in Principal Preparation. *International Journal of Educational Reform, 5*(3), 271–277.

Kaplan, G. (1989). *Who Runs our Schools? The Changing Face of Educational Leadership*. Washington, DC: Institute for Educational Leadership.

King, P. M., & Ketchener, K. S. (1994). *Developing Reflective Judgment*. San Francisco: Jossey-Bass.

Kohn, A. (1993). *Punished by Rewards*. Boston: Houghton Mifflin.

Kotter, J. P. (1998). What Leaders Really Do. *Harvard Business Review on Leadership*. Boston: Harvard Business School Press.

Leithwood, K., & Steinbach, R. (1993). The Relationship Between Variations in Patterns of School Leadership and Group Problem-Solving Processes. In P. Hallinger, K. Leithwood, & J. Murphy (Eds.), *Cognitive Perspectives On Educational Leadership* (pp. 103–129). New York: Teachers College Press.

Leithwood, K., & Steinbach, R. (1995). Expert Problem Solving: Evidence from School and District leaders. Albany, NY: SUNY Press.

Lindblom, C. E. (1959). The Science of Muddling Through. *Public Administration Review*, 19, 79–99.

Lipham, J. M. (1964). Leadership and Administration. In Daniel Griffiths (Ed.), *Behavioral Sciences and Educational Administration. 63rd Yearbook of the National Society for the Study of Education.* Chicago: University of Chicago Press.

Maehr, M. L., & Midgley, C. (1991). Enhancing Student Motivation: A Schoolwide Approach. *Educational Psychologist, 26*(3/4), 399–427.

Marks, H. M., & Louis, K. S. (1997). Does Teacher Empowerment Affect the Classroom? The Implications of Teacher Empowerment for Instructional Practices and Student Academic Performance. *Educational Evaluation and Policy Analysis*, 19, 245–275.

Martin, G. E. (1998). *Intern Manual.* Flagstaff, AZ: Northern Arizona University.

Martin, G. E., Wright, W. F., Perry, E. A., & Amick, J. (2000, Winter). Reaching Your Goals for the Internship: A University Study. *The Journal of the Intermountain Center for Education Effectiveness, 1*(1), 27–32.

Maslow, A. (1954). *Motivation and Personality.* New York: Harper.

McClelland, D. (1961). *The Achieving Society.* New York: Van Nostrand Reinhold.

Milstein, M. M., Bobroff, B. M., & Restine, L. N. (1991). *Internship Programs in Educational Administration: A Guide to Preparing Educational Leaders.* New York: Teachers College Press.

Mintzberg, H. (1989). Mintzberg on Management. New York: Free Press.

Murphy, J. (1992). *The Landscape of Leadership Preparation: Reframing the Education of School Administrators.* Newbury Park, CA: Corwin.

Murphy, J., Shipman, N., & Pearlman, M. (September, 1997). Strengthening Educational Leadership: The ISLLC Standards, Streamlined Seminar, *NAESP, 16*(1).

Muse, I., & Thomas, G. J. (1991). The Rural Principal: Select the Best. *Journal of Rural and Small Schools*, 4(3): 32–37.

National Association of Elementary School Principals. (1990). *Principals for the 21st Century Schools.* Alexandria, VA: Author.

National Association of Secondary School Principals. (1985). *Performance-Based Preparation of Principals: A Framework for Improvement.* Reston, VA: Author.

National Council for Accreditation for Teacher Education. (1995). *Advanced Programs in Educational Leadership for Principals, Superintendents, Curriculum Directors, and Supervisors.* Prepared by the National Policy Board for Educational Administration. Washington, DC: Author.

National Council for Accreditation for Teacher Education. (1994). *NCATE Refined Standards*. Washington DC: Author.

National Council for Accreditation for Teacher Education. (1982). *Standards for the Accreditation of Teacher Education*. Washington DC: Author.

National Policy Board for Educational Administration. (1993). *Principals for our Changing Schools: Knowledge and Skill Base*. Fairfax, VA: Author.

National Council for Professors of Educational Administration. (2000, August). *Panel discussion with Joe Schneider, Neil Shipman, John Hoyle, & Chuck Achilles at the NCPEA Conference*, Ypsilanti, MI.

Rice, M. E., & Schneider, G. T. (1994). A Decade of Teacher Empowerment: An Empirical Analysis of Teacher Involvement in Decision Making, 1980–1991. *Journal of Educational Administration*, 32, 43–58.

Rinehart, J. S., Short, P. M., & Johnson, P. E. (1997). Empowerment and Conflict at School-Based and Non-School-Based Sites in the United States. *Journal of International Studies in Educational Administration*, 25, 77–87.

Rinehart, J. S., Short, P. M., Short, R. J., & Eckley, M. (1998). Teacher Empowerment and Principal Leadership: Understanding the Influence Process. *Educational Administration Quarterly*, 24, 608–30.

Schein, E. H. (1992). *Organizational Culture and Leadership*. San Francisco: Jossey-Bass.

Senge, P., et al. (1996). *The Dance of Change: The Challenges of Sustaining Momentum in Learning Organizations*. New York: Currency Doubleday.

Shulman, L. S. (1986). Paradigms and Research Programs in the Study of Teaching: A Contemporary Perspective. In M. C. Witrock (Ed), *Handbook of Research on Teaching*, (3rd ed). New York: Macmillan.

Simon, H. A. (1947). *Administrative Behavior*. New York: Macmillan.

Taggart, G. L., & Wilson, A. P. (1998). *Promoting Reflective Thinking in Teachers: 44 Action Strategies*. Thousand Oaks, CA: Corwin Press.

Thomas, K. (1976). Conflict and Conflict Management. In M. D. Dunnette (Ed.), *Handbook of Industrial and Organizational Psychology* (pp. 889–936). Chicago: Rand McNally.

University Council for Educational Administration. (1987). *Leaders for America's Schools: The Report of the National Commission on Excellence in Educational Administration*. Tempe, AZ: Author.

Vroom, V. (1964). *Work and Motivation*. New York: Wiley.

Wagner, Tony. (1994). *How Schools Change: Lessons from Three Communities*. Boston: Beacon.

Weiner, B. (1986). *An Attributional Theory of Motivation and Emotion*. New York: Springer.

Yekovich, F. (1993). A Theoretical View of the Development of Expertise in Credit Administration. In P. Hallinger, K. Leithwood, & J. Murphy (Eds.) *Cognitive Perspectives On Educational Leadership* (pp. 146–170). New York: Teachers College Press.

Index